Preface

KU-186-490

'Travel medicine' is a rapidly growing specialty; its aim is to safeguard the health of the traveller, the numbers of whom have recently escalated. It constitutes a relatively recent derivative of the formal 'colonial' discipline of 'tropical medicine'.

Advice to the potential traveller has hitherto tended to focus on *infective* disease. Immunisations have filled a prominent slot, and the traveller who has received his or her 'shots' has felt (often unjustifiably) protected from the hazards and ravages of a tropical or subtropical environment. However, things are not as simple as this! Many diseases and illnesses are *not* in fact *infection*-related; in particular, accidents are an important cause of morbidity in the younger age group, whilst vascular disease exerts its toll in those who are somewhat older. Malaria continues to account for a substantial amount of morbidity and mortality in travellers; however, advice on chemoprophylaxis is becoming increasingly difficult to impart. The 'exotic' diseases, whilst filling substantial sections of textbooks, have a minute place in the 'league table' of travel-associated afflictions.

In this international symposium, organised under the auspices of the Royal College of Physicians of London in June 1994, speakers from many locations gathered in London to discuss various aspects of the increasingly complex subject of travel medicine. Infections of all sorts, from the trivial to the exotic, all received attention, but less frequently addressed topics, for example 'sex-tourism', accidents and the traveller, 'jet lag', and the economic aspects of travel were also discussed. Some of the special problems facing members of the minority ethnic groups in the UK (for example, when they return for a holiday to the land of their birth), and those associated with travel in expatriates and long-term sojourners in the tropics were also well represented in the programme. The day was rounded off with an in-depth overview of preventive strategies for viral hepatitis, that represents a major group of travel-related diseases that will hopefully one day be relegated to medical history.

I am extremely grateful to all the contributors, and to various members of staff of the Royal College of Physicians, especially Anne McSweeney (who organised the minutiae of the conference) and Philada Dann (who, amongst many other tasks, spent many hours chasing up manuscripts for this publication). Dawn Mustafa gave invaluable help with the index. I also thank Dr R H Behrens for valuable suggestions regarding some of the speakers who so admirably covered this crucially important scenario, which falls squarely within the domains of preventive and curative medicine, both of which are encompassed in the overall remit of the Royal College of Physicians.

GORDON C COOK

April 1995

0165241

SbPHA

HKA T
(Co)

✓
SM99004816
3·00
£15·00

TRAVEL-ASSOCIATED DISEASE

*Papers based on a conference organised by
the Royal College of Physicians of London*

Edited by

Gordon C Cook

*President, Royal Society of
Tropical Medicine and Hygiene*

1995

HAROLD BRIDGES LIBRARY
ST MARTINS SERVICES LTD.
LANCASTER

ROYAL COLLEGE OF PHYSICIANS OF LONDON

1860160123

Acknowledgements

The Royal College of Physicians acknowledges with thanks a grant from the Virgin Healthcare Foundation towards the cost of producing this book.

Royal College of Physicians of London
11 St Andrews Place, London NW1 4LE

Registered Charity No. 210508

Copyright © 1995 Royal College of Physicians of London
ISBN 1 86016 012 3

Typeset by Dan-Set Graphics, Telford, Shropshire
Printed in Great Britain by The Lavenham Press Ltd, Lavenham, Sudbury, Suffolk

Contributors

Ronald H Behrens MD BSc MRCP(UK) MRCS *Consultant Physician, Hospital for Tropical Diseases Travel Clinic, St Pancras Way, London NW1 0PE*

David J Bradley MA DM FRCP FRCPath FFPHM *Professor of Tropical Hygiene in the University of London and Co-Director of the PHLS Malaria Reference Laboratory, Department of Epidemiology and Population Sciences, London School of Hygiene and Tropical Medicine, Keppel Street, London WC1E 7HT*

Rodney Y Cartwright MB FRCPath *Consultant Microbiologist and Director, Public Health Laboratory, St Luke's Hospital, Guildford GU1 3NT*

Gordon C Cook MD DSc FRCP FRACP FLS *Consultant Physician, Hospital for Tropical Diseases, St Pancras Way, London NW1 0PE*

Richard J Fairhurst MB MRCS DObstRCOG *Director of the Travellers Medical Service; Consultant in Accident & Emergency Medicine, University College Hospital, Grafton Way, London WC1E 6AU*

Michael JG Farthing MD FRCP *Professor of Gastroenterology, Digestive Diseases Research Centre, The Medical College of St Bartholomew's Hospital, Charterhouse Square, London EC1M 6BQ*

David R Hill MD *Division of Infectious Diseases, University of Connecticut Health Center, Farmington, CT 06030-3212 USA; formerly: Hospital for Tropical Diseases Travel Clinic, St Pancras Way, London NW1 0PE*

Dieter Kleiber *Professor and Head of the Department of Health Prevention, Psychological Institute, Freie Universität Berlin, Habelschwerdter Allee 45, 14 195 Berlin, Germany*

Anthony N Nicholson OBE QHS DSc FRCP(Ed) FRCPath FRAeS RAF *Consultant Adviser in Aviation Medicine (Royal Air Force) and Commandant, Royal Air Force School of Aviation Medicine, Farnborough, Hampshire GU14 6SZ*

Daniel Reid OBE MD FRCP(Glas) FFPHM DPH *Honorary Professor in the University of Glasgow and Director of the Scottish Centre for Infection and Environmental Health, Ruchill Hospital, Glasgow G22 9NB*

Robert Steffen MD *Professor and Head of the Division of Communicable Diseases, Institut für Sozial und Preventivmedizin der Universität Zurich, CH 80006 Zurich, Switzerland*

William RC Weir MB FRCP *Honorary Senior Lecturer in Infectious Diseases, Royal Free Hospital School of Medicine and Consultant Physician, Coppetts Wood Hospital, Coppetts Road, Muswell Hill, London N10 1JN*

Martin Wilke *Academic Assistant, Institute for Intercultural Education, Freie Universität Berlin, Habelschwerdter Allee 45, 14 195 Berlin, Germany*

Arie J Zuckerman MD DSc FRCP FRCPath *Dean and Professor of Medical Microbiology, Royal Free Hospital School of Medicine, Rowland Hill Street, London NW3 2PF*

Contents

*Royal College of Physicians lecture delivered on 22 June 1994.

1 | Epidemiology of travel-related diseases

Daniel Reid

Director, Scottish Centre for Infection and Environmental Health,
Ruchill Hospital, Glasgow; Honorary Professor, University of Glasgow

The hazards of travel have been recognised for centuries by the soldier, the missionary and the trader. Military campaigns have been badly affected by illness and unhealthy areas have become 'out-of-bounds' for those going abroad for commercial purposes.

In more recent times, the number of people travelling abroad has increased dramatically. Groups now contributing to this increase include tourists, business travellers, technical experts, pilgrims, migrant workers, refugees, immigrants, military personnel, political representatives, sporting participants and spectators, and the travel support services. Of particular significance has been the growth of the 'package tour', although recently this form of travel has received some setbacks: in 1986, in the UK the percentage of package holiday visits was 54%, whereas by 1989 this had fallen to 41%.

The advent of the aeroplane has also been a major factor in increasing the number of travellers. Between 1949 and 1989 there was a 16-fold increase in the number of international arrivals at UK airports, a 37-fold increase in the number of scheduled air passengers and an 18-fold increase in the number of UK residents travelling abroad; the proportion of those travelling beyond Europe has increased 48-fold. International tourist arrivals in North America have also increased spectacularly, with 6,180,000 in 1950 and more than 55 million in 1990. In 1949, 26 million international tourists were recorded (Table 1), whereas by 1990 this had risen to 429 million, with 30% of those travelling to the Mediterranean area. If domestic tourists are included, it has been estimated by the World Tourism Organisation that the world total for arrivals at all destinations is now approximately 4,150 million.

Not only has the number of travellers increased but also the destinations to which passenger aircraft now fly. Moreover, the time taken to travel from one country to another has shortened considerably;

1

Table 1. Growth in international travel

	1949 (millions)	1960 (millions)	1970 (millions)	1990 (millions)
International tourists	26	72	201	429
Air travellers throughout the world	31	106	386	1,160
Visits abroad by UK residents	1.7	6	11.8	31*

*1989 figures

between 1948 and the present time, the fastest passenger aircraft cruising speed has risen from 340 to 1,356 miles per hour (in Concorde). This has increased the hazard even more as, paradoxically, the slower sea passages had a measure of safety as they ensured that the incubation periods of many infections were completed during the voyage, thus allowing appropriate surveillance measures, vaccination of contacts etc. to be undertaken before the destination was reached. Today, air passengers can arrive from the tropics still asymptomatic even though they have contracted an infection during their stay abroad.

Studies on package tourists

In 1973, an outbreak of pneumonia with three fatalities occurred in a group of package holiday-makers returning from Benidorm, Spain to Glasgow, Scotland; this was subsequently attributed to legionnaires' disease.[1,2] This example of travellers returning with a previously unknown disease motivated the development of a series of multidisciplinary collaborative studies of illnesses associated with travel,[3] conducted by the Scottish Centre for Infection and Environmental Health (SCIEH), the University of Glasgow Department of Infectious Diseases, the Department of Laboratory Medicine and the Regional Virus Laboratory, all situated at Ruchill Hospital, Glasgow.

Over the past 15 years the SCIEH has established a system both to monitor the health experience of returning Scottish travellers and to make specific enquiries into groups of travellers identified as being 'at risk' following an alert about a possible health problem. Analysis was carried out on the information provided by travellers using a 20-item standard questionnaire[4] asking for personal and travel data, with a pre-paid reply envelope addressed to the SCIEH. Of a total of 14,227 respondents, 37% gave a history of illness with response rates ranging from 21%[5] to 77%[6] among the component study groups. The attack rates ranged from a low 19% amongst summer visitors to Scotland in 1980 and 20% among holiday-makers on winter package tours[7], to 75% of those on summer package tours to Romania in 1981[8] and 78% of 375 tourists returning from Spain (who selected themselves for study by writing or telephoning to the SCIEH[9] following media publicity on legionellosis and travel in 1977).

The distribution of travellers by age groups and illness (Table 2) shows that the highest attack rates were recorded by the under-40 age groups, with 41% of the 10–19 age group and 48% of the 20–29 age group reporting illness. Thereafter, attack rates show a progressive diminution with increasing age. Eighteen per cent of the travellers reported alimentary symptoms, predominantly diarrhoea and vomiting. If all the symptom complexes which include alimentary symptoms are considered, this figure rises to 28% of the total number of travellers and 76% of all those who reported illness.

If the attack rates are compared in terms of the countries visited, there is a general trend that the further south and, to some extent, the further east the travel, the higher the rate for UK residents (Table 3). This remains generally true both in summer and in winter. Examples in support of this trend are the 77% attack rate reported by tourists to North Africa in the summer, the 57% rate for those travelling to eastern Europe and the 32% attack rate

Table 2. Age of travellers and reports of illness

Age group (years)	Total	Unwell (%)
0–9	550	33
10–19	1,974	41
20–29	3,033	48
30–39	2,028	38
40–49	2,297	32
50–59	2,381	28
60 +	1,239	20
not known	725	32
Total	14,227	37

Table 3. Area visited, season and reports of illness

Area visited	Attack rate	
	Summer (%)	Winter (%)
Europe (north)	19	20
Europe (east)	57	12
Mediterranean (southern Europe)	34	19
Mediterranean (north Africa)	77	32
Average attack rate:	*37*	*20*

reported by winter tourists to North Africa. In addition, attack rates were substantially lower in the winter than summer, the mean rate for winter travellers being 20%[7] compared with 37% for summer travellers.

Mortality

A review of 952 Scots who died while abroad between 1973 and 1988[10] revealed that infection accounted for only a small proportion (4%) of the mortality; cardiovascular disease was the most frequently recorded cause of death (69%) followed by accidents and injuries (21%). Most deaths occurred in the 50–59 years age range (50%), with the highest cardiovascular mortality (34%) in the 60–69 years range, and the highest death rate from accidents and injuries (32%) in the 20–29 years group. This highlights the risk of a strenuous holiday in a warm climate for older people with pre-existing cardiovascular problems. It also demonstrates the potential for prevention of deaths in younger travellers by improving awareness of hazards such as road accidents and swimming, to which alcohol is a frequent contributing factor.

Further evidence that lifestyle has a bearing on travellers' problems is the finding that 37% of 2,748 smokers reported illness compared with 32% of 7,294 non-smokers — a statistically significant difference. No significant correlation was noted between travellers reporting illness and the reason for travel, the type of accommodation used, the traveller's socio-economic status or the length of stay abroad, although the highest attack rates were recorded in those who were unskilled or unemployed and in those who set off with

Table 4. Reports of AIDS and HIV infection in Scotland contracted abroad (data to September 1992)

	Total no. of cases	Infections contracted abroad	
		(total)	(%)
All AIDS cases	324	21	6.5
AIDS cases known to be heterosexually acquired	33	19	57.6
All HIV cases	1845	50	2.7
HIV cases known to be heterosexually acquired	117	48	41.0

pre-existing ill health. In recent years, the threat to tourists of contracting AIDS whilst abroad has caused great concern. An analysis of the Scottish data indicates that infection derived from outside the UK is undoubtedly occurring (Table 4).

Laboratory information

Analysis of laboratory isolates of pathogens in travellers collected at the SCIEH reveals that between 1975 and 1986 there has been a five-fold increase in the annual total number of reports and a proportionate rise from 62% to 90% relating to holiday-makers[11,12] (improved reporting may be a contributory factor to this increase). The isolates in those visiting southern Europe comprised 45% of the total in 1986 compared with 26% in 1975; there is a less proportionate change for those visiting other areas. A cumulative review of the pathogens isolated shows that infections associated with inadequate food handling and poor water supply or sanitation account for 87% of these reports (total, 4,921).

Other surveys

Published surveys from various researchers show a gastrointestinal illness attack rate of:

- 28% in a study of 16,568 randomly selected Swiss travellers;[13]
- 18% of 2,665 Finnish travellers;[14]
- 30% of UK tourists to Benidorm;[15] and
- 41% of 2,184 Scottish holiday-makers.[16]

All the studies which specify the most affected age group were in agreement (ie 20–29 years) and, similarly, where the area was specific, travel to north Africa or eastern Europe produced the highest attack rates.

The broad correlation of these various findings lends credibility to attempts to detect patterns of illness derived from the travellers studied, and the use of largely identical methodologies encourages a comparative analysis of relative risk of illness to the travellers (Table 5).

Cost of travel-related illness

From information supplied by 3,409 travellers from the UK who became unwell whilst abroad, 1% required hospital admission on their return and 14% consulted a doctor. The cost per travel-associated hospital admission in the UK in 1985 was given as approximately £550 (US$1,000). If the survey figures for Scottish travellers are used as a basis for calculating the total cost of admission to hospital for all ill travellers, it is estimated that in 1986 it was over £11 million (US$20 million) in the UK. There is no reason to suppose that this total will have decreased since then. This does not take into account the considerable additional costs involved with primary care consultations, laboratory investigations, specialist consultations, drug prescriptions, loss both of working days and of vacation time due to such illness, and, of course, the considerable expense incurred by travellers and their insurance companies from medical treatment obtained abroad.[17]

Conclusions

Studies conducted during the past 20 years allow several broad conclusions:

Table 5. Profile of travellers at risk

Package holidaymakers	> other travellers
Inexperienced travellers	> other travellers
Travellers going further south, particularly north Africa	> other travellers
Summer travellers	> winter travellers
Younger age groups (specifically 20–29 years)	> older travellers
Smokers	> non-smokers

- young travellers experience more illness;
- the greater the climatic and cultural contrast between the traveller's country of origin and the destination country, the higher the risk;
- by far the commonest afflictions the traveller is likely to experience are diarrhoea and vomiting; and
- the cost of travel-related illness in the UK is in excess of £11 million.

Acknowledgements

The help of Mrs Margaret McInnes, Dr Jonathon Cossar, Miss Patricia Cassels, Miss Fiona Johnston, Mr Andrew Millar and Dr David Goldberg in the preparation of this chapter is greatly appreciated.

References

1. Reid D, Grist NR, Najera RJ. Illness associated with package tours: a combined Spanish-Scottish study. *Bulletin of the World Health Organization* 1978; **56**: 117–22
2. Lawson JH, Grist NR, Reid D, Wilson TS. Legionnaires' disease. *Lancet* 1977; **ii**: 108
3. Reid D, Dewar RD, Fallon RJ, Cossar JH, Grist NR. Infection and travel: the experience of package tourists and other travellers. *Journal of Infection* 1980; **2**: 365–70
4. Cossar JH, Reid D, Fallon RJ, Bell EJ, *et al*. A cumulative review of studies on travellers, their experience of illness and the implications of these findings. *Journal of Infection* 1990; **21**: 27–42
5. Dewar RD, Cossar JH, Reid D, Grist NR. Illness amongst travellers to Scotland: a pilot study. *Health Bulletin (Edinburgh)* 1983; **41** (No. 3): 155–62
6. Cossar JH, Dewar RD, Fallon RJ, Reid D, *et al*. Rapid response health surveillance of Scottish tourists. *Travel and Traffic Medicine International* 1984; **2**: 123–7
7. Cossar JH, Dewar RD, Reid D, Grist NR. Travel and health: illness associated with winter package holidays. *Journal of the Royal College of General Practitioners* 1988; **33**: 642–5
8. Grist NR, Cossar JH, Reid D. Illness associated with a package holiday in Romania. *Scottish Medical Journal* 1985; **30**: 156–60
9. Cossar JH, Dewar RD, Fallon RJ, Grist NR, Reid D. *Legionella pneumophila* in tourists. *Practitioner* 1982; **226**: 1543–8
10. Paixao MTD'A, Dewar RD, Cossar JH, Covell RG, Reid D. What do Scots die of when abroad? *Scottish Medical Journal* 1991; **36**: 114–6
11. Sharp JCM. Imported infection into Scotland, 1975. *Communicable Disease Scotland Weekly Report* 76/26, v–vi
12. Campbell DM. Imported infection into Scotland, 1986. *Communicable Disease Scotland Weekly Report* 87/47, 7–8

13. Steffen R, van der Linde F, Gyr K, Schär M. Epidemiology of diarrhea in travelers. *Journal of the American Medical Association* 1983; **249**: 1176–80

14. Peltolar H, Kyronseppa H, Holsa P. Trips to the South — a health hazard. *Scandinavian Journal of Infectious Diseases* 1983; **15**: 375–81

15. Cartwright RY. Holiday infections surveyed. *PHLS Microbiology Digest* 1987; **4**: 1415

16. McEwan A, Jackson MH. Illness among Scots holidaymakers who had travelled abroad, summer 1983. *Communicable Diseases Scotland Weekly Report* 87/16, 7–9

17. Reid D, Cossar JH. The size of the problem. In: *Travellers' Health* 3rd ed (ed. Dawood R). Oxford: Oxford University Press, 1992: 8–14

2 | Malaria in travellers: epidemiology, disease and environment

David J Bradley
Professor of Tropical Hygiene, University of London; Co-Director, Public Health Laboratory Service Malaria Reference Laboratory

Malaria in travellers is in effect a biased microcosm of malaria in the world as a whole; its understanding requires some grasp of the global epidemiology of malaria plus the special features of travel and travellers. Of the 200 million cases of malaria worldwide each year, 2,000 (about one in 100,000) are manifested in the UK so that British malaria is the small tip of a very large iceberg. Yet it comprises 2,000 serious and potential fatal illnesses (Table 1), an average of seven deaths per year—almost all of which are preventable tragedies, and the potential for vastly increased numbers of cases (and deaths) if present efforts at prevention are relaxed. Moreover, both the prevention of cases and the management of those that occur are becoming annually more complex and difficult. This chapter will necessarily present an oversimplified picture of current realities. Three aspects will be addressed:

- the determinants of risk of malaria infection for travellers, including the effects of drug resistance;

Table 1. Imported cases of malaria reported in the UK

Year	No. of cases	*Plasmodium falciparum* infections	No. of deaths
1987	1,816	724	7
1988	1,674	1,051	7
1989	1,987	1,117	4
1990	2,096	1,097	4
1991	2,332	1,314	12
1992	1,629	972	10
1993	1,922	1,077	5
7-year total	13,456	7,352	49

- the appropriate responses for the protection of travellers; and
- a brief consideration of emerging and future issues.

Risk determinants

The risk determinants of malaria are diverse, and are briefly classified in Table 2. The overwhelming practical aspect is *awareness* of
risk: awareness by travellers, their doctors and other health advi-
sors, and travel agents. Once the possibility of malaria is considered
in those who are unwell, parasitological diagnosis is not difficult,
and treatment of uncomplicated malaria completely feasible. The
risk of malaria is a real one for travellers to countries endemic for
malaria, even if all precautions against mosquito bites and appropriate chemoprophylaxis have been complied with. This awareness
of risk is crucial for reducing the mortality of imported malaria.

Geographical and seasonal factors

Malaria occurs throughout the tropics and much of the subtropics,
but the risk is extremely variable. Substantial areas are free of
malaria because:

- they are too dry;
- they are at too high an altitude (hence cool);
- it has been *eradicated* (this includes all Europe and the USA,
  and many Caribbean islands);
- it has been *controlled;* or
- anopheline vector *mosquitoes are naturally absent* (as in the Poly-
  nesian islands).

Even within malarious areas the chance of becoming infected
varies greatly and depends upon the ecology of the local vector
mosquitoes. If they feed frequently—preferentially on people

Table 2. Determinants of malaria risk for travellers from the UK

Place being visited	Transmission levels of place
	Time of year
Person travelling	Innate and acquired resistance
	Behaviour
Parasite involved	Species composition
	Levels of drug resistance
Protective measures taken	Against mosquito bites
	Against infection

rather than animals, are numerous, and particularly if they belong
to a long-lived anopheline species, the level of transmission will be
high (Fig 1). It may be one hundred or even one thousand times
greater than in an area where malaria is *just* endemic but with few

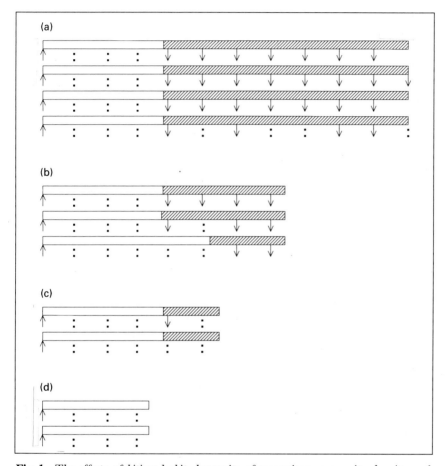

Fig 1. *The effects of biting habit, longevity of mosquitoes, mosquito density and
duration of parasite development cycle upon malaria transmission.* Each bar represents the life of a mosquito from when it catches malaria (shaded part
of bar = presence of sporozoites in the salivary glands; white part =
absence of sporozoites); ↑ = a bite that infects a mosquito with malaria;
↓ = an infectious bite from a mosquito that may infect man; : = a bite that
is non-infectious either because the mosquito lacks sporozoites in its salivary glands or because it bites a domestic animal. a) several long-lived
mosquitoes that usually feed on man are infected;   26 subsequent bites
capable of transmitting malaria; b) mosquitoes with moderate longevity
which sometimes feed on animals; nine potentially infective bites; c) few
mosquitoes, with short lives which feed mainly on animals; a single bite is
infective to man; d) very short-lived mosquitoes, unable to transmit
malaria.

and short-lived vectors that feed infrequently and mainly upon domestic stock.

The highest levels of risk are encountered in parts of sub-Saharan Africa, where mosquitoes of the *Anopheles gambiae* complex are the most effective known vectors of malaria; an unprotected person in rural Tanzania may receive an average of one infective mosquito bite nightly. This pattern is seen in areas of west, central and east Africa. The indigenous inhabitants are repeatedly infected from infancy; those who survive to adulthood will have slowly acquired partial immunity — especially against illness due to malaria — but at the price of a massive infant mortality. The risk to tourists staying in air-conditioned accommodation will be less, but it is still high and it would be folly not to take precautions against being bitten as well as chemoprophylaxis. Moreover, the UK tourist will usually be non-immune and therefore have a much greater risk of a fatal outcome.

By contrast, in an endemic area of Asia, the risk may be much lower and the local inhabitants may get on average an infective bite once or twice a year. This still suffices to produce many clinical cases of malaria, and for the disease to be a substantial public health problem locally. For the traveller who visits the area for a short time, however, the risk is very much lower than in Africa. There may be marked variations between different ecological zones within a country. For example, the central plain of Thailand is relatively free of intense malaria transmission even without the control measures that are now in place. In contrast, the border areas which combine forested hills, illegal logging and gem-mining activities that create mosquito breeding sites, much trans-border migration, and de-forestation that creates a mosaic of sun and shade and small streams support *Anopheles dirus* and *Anopheles minimus* (both efficient vectors of *Plasmodium falciparum* malaria). However, the risk is predomi-nantly to those in or near the forest under cover of darkness, and falls on local smugglers and refugees rather than on most travellers from Europe.

Transmission is often markedly seasonal, either because the winter is too cold for parasite development within the mosquito or because it is too dry for mosquitoes to find water to breed. Very hot, dry weather may also shorten mosquito life dramatically.

High-risk groups

Some travellers to malarious areas are at a much greater risk of contracting malaria than others. The business traveller or urban tourist who stays in an air-conditioned hotel in the capital will be at low risk, except in some African cities which retain breeding sites for *Anopheles gambiae,* and in those south Asian cities with the urban tank-breeding *Anopheles stephensi* which is an effective malaria vector. The highly polluted water of many urban areas supports the breeding of culicine mosquitoes rather than anophelines, which usually prefer cleaner water. Business travellers may sometimes be at high risk if their work takes them into rural areas, or if their host proposes a day at the local game park — which may be much more malarious than the city.

The package tourist to an African coast resort may be at high malaria risk (though one to an equivalent resort in Thailand may have *no* risk). The highest levels of risk are encountered by overland travellers who may go off the beaten track and spend several months in rural areas with high malaria endemicity — far from good medical advice. If they are sleeping rough or in unscreened accommodation, the use of insecticide-impregnated bed-nets may be an important source of protection at night.

The largest single group of travellers among the cases of imported malaria comprises immigrants well settled in the UK but who return to their country/area of origin to visit friends and relations (see Chapter 9). There are two main subgroups: first, a south Asian population originating from India and Pakistan who predominantly contract *P. vivax* malaria, though *P. falciparum* malaria is seen in about 14% of cases and was responsible for two deaths in 1992–93. The second group, which has emerged only recently as numerically important, comprises west Africans settled mainly in London and returning to Nigeria, Ghana and Sierra Leone. Few are believed to take chemoprophylaxis, and estimates by Gair (personal communication) suggest that this group has a greatly increased malaria risk — above other population groups or travellers. The case fatality rate in this last group is 0.6%, which is substantially lower than for other tourists and businessmen, whose case fatality rate is 1.2–1.4% if infected with *P. falciparum,* suggesting a possible degree of residual acquired immunity sufficient to reduce mortality from malaria but not morbidity.

Three groups of overseas visitors to the UK contribute to the burden of imported malaria:

- visitors who originate from, or who have previously been to endemic countries;
- new immigrants (now much less than a decade ago); and
- UK citizens who have been living in malarious countries and are visiting the UK — this group appears to be at special risk.

Plasmodium spp

There are four human malaria parasites, but the majority of imported infections are due to *P. vivax* or *P. falciparum*. *P. vivax* was the predominant parasite when records commenced until 1987, but the number of cases of *P. falciparum* malaria has steadily increased because of changing travel patterns, resistance of the parasite to chemoprophylaxis, and resurgence in the malarious countries of Asia. *P. falciparum* cases now comprise about 56% of the parasites encountered — an ominous development since *P. falciparum* malaria is responsible for almost all the fatalities in the UK.

P. vivax malaria predominates in cases originating from Asia (for examples see Table 3). Until recently, chloroquine chemoprophylaxis prevented illness from *P. vivax* malaria, but many cases occurred several months after return to the UK because of persistent hypnozoites in the liver developing subsequent to the cessation of prophylaxis. Chloroquine resistance is now beginning to be found in some Asian strains of *P. vivax* malaria. In west Africa, where the indigenous inhabitants are genetically resistant to *P. vivax*, the clinically similar *P. ovale* is often found; however, *P. falciparum* strongly predominates, as in the rest of sub-Saharan Africa.

Table 3. Malaria cases: the ten countries providing most cases of imported malaria over a six-year period (76% of all imported malaria and 75% of *P. falciparum* infection, with India and Pakistan accounting for 74% of imported *P. vivax* cases)

Country	No. of cases	*P. falciparum* infection	*P. vivax* infection
India	2,360	153	2,168
Nigeria	2,097	1,746	35
Ghana	1,165	1,028	19
Pakistan	1,142	39	1,089
Kenya	755	632	56
Uganda	267	222	10
Sierra Leone	231	193	9
Zambia	190	161	4
Malawi	176	142	16
Tanzania	163	122	23
All cases	11,319	5,936	4,394

Resistance to chemoprophylaxis

Resistance of *P. falciparum* to the commonly used prophylactic drugs is the greatest current problem in malaria prevention. Chloroquine resistance has spread from its origins on the Thai-Vietnam border and Colombia to encompass most of the world in the last 40 years. In those countries where chloroquine resistance developed early, other compounds have been in use for prolonged periods, and multidrug resistance is a substantial and increasing problem. This is most notable in south-east Asia where, in parts of Cambodia and on the Thai-Cambodian border, for example, up to 40% of *P. falciparum* strains are resistant to mefloquine as well as to most other antimalarials. Chloroquine-resistant *P. falciparum* malaria is now prevalent throughout the highly endemic areas of sub-Saharan Africa, the Amazon basin, east Asia and Oceania, and many parts of south Asia. Table 4 indicates the scale of resistance to the commoner malaria parasites globally.

Table 4. Resistance to chemoprophylaxis: an indication of the relative frequency of resistance to the commoner antimalarials worldwide

	P. falciparum infection	*P. vivax* infection
Pyrimethamine	++++	
Chloroquine	+++	+
Proguanil ('Paludrine')	++	
'Fansidar' (pyrimethamine/sulfadoxine)	++	
Quinine	+	
Mefloquine	+	

Recommendations for prophylaxis (see also Chapter 11)

What, then, are the key protective measures to be taken? They are expressed simply in Table 5.

Table 5. The four cardinal points of malaria prevention in travellers

1. Awareness of risk
2. Avoidance of bites
3. Compliance with chemoprophylaxis
4. Awareness of risk again

1. Awareness of risk is fundamental because it provides motivation for compliance with advice. Detailed risks by area are available in both the standard UK advice[1] and the Ministry of Health *Yellow Book*.

2. Avoidance of bites from anopheline mosquitoes is the first line of defence and often receives inadequate attention. Biting occurs between dusk and dawn, often with a concentration during the night. Consequently, protection is afforded either by sleeping in well screened (preferably air-conditioned) rooms that have been sprayed with a 'knock-down' insecticide in early evening or by sleeping under a bed-net impregnated with synthetic pyrethroids. Such bed-nets have recently been shown to give substantial protection even to the inhabitants of highly endemic areas.[2] Infants may be similarly protected throughout the period of biting. The main remaining opportunity for adults to get bitten is between dusk and bedtime, and the risk may be reduced by the use of repellents such as diethyl-toluamide (DEET) applied to exposed skin or to clothes and by wearing loose-fitting clothing over otherwise exposed skin areas.

3. Appropriate chemoprophylaxis is the third protective measure, the most important aspect of which is compliance (Fig. 2). There is much discussion of alternative regimens, but the great majority of malaria deaths are in people who have taken no prophylaxis or have taken it irregularly. Early cessation of the regimen on returning to the UK is a particular problem. Chemoprophylaxis needs to be taken from one week before departure until four weeks after return.

4. The fourth, and most important protective measure to reduce mortality from imported malaria is for patient and doctor to be aware that no regimen can provide 100% protection, and that any febrile episode or 'flu-like' illness within a year (especially within the first three months) after returning to the UK must be considered as possible malaria and investigated as a medical emergency.

The choice of a prophylactic antimalarial is set out in the UK recommendations. Where chloroquine-resistant *P. falciparum* malaria is absent, chloroquine alone gives good protection; in the presence of mild to moderate chloroquine resistance, the combination of daily proguanil and weekly chloroquine has given substantial protection — and still does in many areas. Its other advantages have been the absence of mortality from the drug, the long experience with it, and safety for children and pregnant women.

A much more recently introduced antimalarial, mefloquine, gives a higher level of protection against chloroquine-resistant malaria, and cumulative experience is leading to a relaxation of the previously strict limitations on its use. The main concern in the

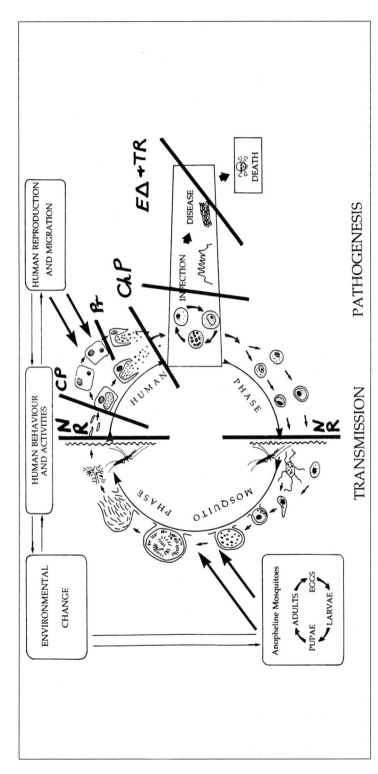

Fig 2. *The malaria parasite life-cycle and prevention of malaria in travellers.* **a.** prevention of mosquito bites by bed-nets (N) and repellents (R); **b.** chemoprophylaxis acting to prevent infection reaching the liver; causal prophylaxis (CP), killing hypnozoites in the liver (primaquine (Pr)), or preventing blood stages (eg chloroquine (Ch), proguanil (P)); **c.** early diagnosis and treatment of clinical malaria (EΔ and TR).

UK has been the perceived frequency of neuropsychiatric side-effects. Formal surveys in Europe have shown a low incidence of disconcerting symptoms, including anxiety, nightmares, psychotic attacks and convulsions. A survey frequency has been found of one in 10,000, but these symptoms have been seen more frequently by many practitioners. Confidence in mefloquine has increased steadily, and there is now evidence that it can be taken for up to 1–2 years without increased side-effects, nor are there problems with taking mefloquine during the second and third trimesters of pregnancy, though both epilepsy and a history of a serious psychiatric disorder are definite contra-indications. Mefloquine has been the preferred antimalarial for east Africa and part of central Africa since 1993, and current opinion is that it is recommended for all the more malarious areas of sub-Saharan Africa, with the combination of proguanil and chloroquine as an alternative for those unable to take mefloquine. In many areas of south-east Asia, where risk is relatively low and multiple drug resistance common, chemoprophylaxis is inappropriate. In areas of high transmission and a great deal of mefloquine resistance, the use of doxycycline has provided good protection, particularly to UN forces working in Cambodia. Detailed recommendations are available. It is necessary to reiterate that 'breakthrough' malaria is seen on all regimens that have been used — even though uncommonly.

In several countries much visited by tourists, although there is endemic malaria, the risk to travellers from the UK is very low (Table 6). In these circumstances, chemoprophylaxis may still be appropriate for the areas of greatest risk within the countries, provided that the parasites are sensitive to chloroquine or another 'safe' antimalarial.

The main difficulties in practice with chemoprophylaxis arise in those with concomitant health problems, especially the young.

Table 6. Countries with areas of endemic malaria which yield relatively few cases in UK travellers. (The six-year database is the same as that used in Table 3)

Country	No. of cases	*P. falciparum* infection
Egypt	0	0
Turkey	4	0
Thailand	54	14
Bali	4	1

Travellers with epilepsy should not take mefloquine and, less certainly, chloroquine. For those going to very high risk areas, doxycycline might be considered, but this is unsuitable for children, and 'Maloprim' (dapsone/pyrimethamine fixed combination) may give limited protection. A further difficulty is that the half-life of doxycycline is shortened in those on anticonvulsants, but the consequences of raising the dose have not been reported. Further difficulties in malaria chemoprophylaxis arise in those with marked renal or hepatic impairment, when dose modification is needed or choice of an antimalarial that is mainly handled by the more functional organ. Splenectomy greatly increases the risk of severe malaria and full chemoprophylaxis is essential.

Given that no regimen of prophylaxis and avoidance of bites is totally effective, and that there are other areas with a low risk of malaria but a relatively high chance that any infection will be due to a strain of multiply resistant *P. falciparum,* it has been recommended that travellers to places inaccessible to medical care should carry drugs for 'standby' treatment in the event of a fever. Three problems have relatively recently become evident with 'standby' therapy. First, there has been a tendency to overprescribe. 'Standby' treatment is appropriate for only a small number of travellers far from the beaten track or to countries where the doctors and pharmacies are likely to lack the appropriate chemotherapy. Secondly, with increasing levels of resistance of the parasites to multiple drugs, the choice of 'standby' agent is difficult, especially in south-east Asia; relevant issues are briefly addressed in the UK guidelines. 'Fansidar' (a fixed combination of pyrimethamine and sulfadoxine) is the most convenient single-dose, 'standby' treatment where effective, but in south-east Asia several days of quinine followed by tetracycline or 'Fansidar' may be needed. Thirdly, although halofantrine appeared initially to be a useful 'standby' drug, it is no longer recommended for this use in remote places because of its cardiotoxicity, especially in those who already have a prolonged QT_c interval.

Summary and conclusions

Summarising risk and prevention: awareness, avoidance of mosquito bites and chemoprophylaxis are needed, but prompt diagnosis and treatment of subsequent febrile attacks are especially important. Countries much visited and at high risk are shown in Table 3, but the origins of fatalities (Table 7) are of special significance. Kenya is the major scenario of fatal cases, often in tourists; west Africa is also notorious.

Table 7. Source of infection in 45 individuals who died as a result of malaria in a six-year period. (The database is the same as that used in Table 3)

Source	Deaths	
	No.	%
Kenya	18	40
Nigeria	7	16
Ghana	6	13
India	2	4
Gambia	2	4
Zimbabwe	2	4
Others	8	18
Total	*45*	

What are likely to be the changes in available antimalarials? Few new drugs are in an advanced state of development, except for the qinghaosu derivatives such as artemether. Some of these are already becoming available, especially in the forested areas of south-east Asia where they are most needed. There is concern that they are beginning to reach Africa, where they are not yet strictly necessary as other selected drugs remain effective. The qinghaosu derivatives are for treatment and *not* prophylaxis; they are excreted rapidly and may give rise to neurotoxicity on repeated use.

Hopes for better protection of travellers in the future focus increasingly upon the prospects for a vaccine. The Colombian merozoite antigen vaccine, which gave about 50% protection in a controlled trial in South America, is now being assessed in Tanzania, The Gambia and Thailand under conditions of varying malaria transmission levels; results are eagerly awaited.

In the longer term, there has been speculation that gradual climatic change ('global warming') may increase the potential for malaria transmission within the UK. In broad terms, an increase in temperature will shorten the duration of the extrinsic cycle of the malaria parasite in the mosquito and, provided the changes in temperature and humidity do not also shorten mosquito life, facilitate transmission. Suitable anophelines to transmit *P. vivax* already exist in the UK, but there is more uncertainty about their capacity to transmit African strains of *P. falciparum*. However, climate is not the limiting factor for the current endemicity of malaria in Europe; although it is unlikely that climatic change would be permitted to have a major effect upon the occurrence of malaria transmission in the UK, it may well increase the number of imported cases. In such an event, steps would be taken to control any secondary cases by means of insecticides or treatment of newly arrived people.

References

1. Bradley DJ. Malaria Reference Laboratory and the Ross Institute. Prophylaxis against malaria for travellers from the United Kingdom. *British Medical Journal* 1993; **306**: 1247–52
2. Snow RW, Hayes RJ, Greenwood BM,. Permethrin treated bednets prevent malaria in Gambian children. *Transactions of the Royal Society of Tropical Medicine and Hygiene* 1988; **82**: 838–42

3 | Travellers' diarrhoea

Michael JG Farthing

Professor of Gastroenterology, St Bartholomew's Hospital, London

Diarrhoea is the most common ailment associated with travel (see also Chapter 4). More than 30% of individuals travelling from developed to developing countries can expect to suffer an episode of diarrhoea during their trip or shortly after their return.[1-3] A conservative estimate suggests that there are more than 10 million episodes of travellers' diarrhoea (TD) each year, most of which, fortunately, are mild, self-limiting and more inconvenient than medically hazardous. However, diarrhoea in travellers provokes considerable anxiety and may result in significant disruption of vacation, business or other travel plans. There are considerable economic implications for the host country, since the threat of an illness may make some travellers disinclined to visit those high-risk regions of the world, and thus reduce potential income from tourism. Health risks may also be a negative factor influencing decisions regarding foreign investment and business ventures in these locations. TD can be a serious and even life-threatening illness in a minority of travellers.

What is this syndrome?

TD is usually defined as the passage of three or more unformed stools in 24 hours during or shortly after travel, or any number of loose stools when associated with fever, abdominal pain or vomiting.[1] Passage of any number of dysenteric stools (diarrhoea with blood) associated with travel is also included in the definition. Some recent controlled therapeutic studies in TD have modified the entry criteria by enrolling subjects who have had a single watery stool. This has permitted the assessment of antibiotic interventions early in the course of the illness, while the placebo group has confirmed the typical natural history of TD.

The most common presentation of TD is acute watery diarrhoea. Symptoms may begin at any time during travel or shortly after return, but the illness most commonly occurs early in the trip, the peak onset being on the third day of travel.[3] Most cases of

23

watery diarrhoea (75%) have less than six stools per 24 hours but severity is highly variable. Untreated, the mean duration of TD is four days, with a median of two days. In 1% of sufferers symptoms persist for more than one month. Other associated symptoms include anorexia, nausea, vomiting, abdominal cramps, flatulence and bloating. Fever is unusual and, when present, usually low grade. Dehydration is typically mild and may not be clinically evident. However, infants, young children and the elderly are more susceptible to the effects of dehydration and acidosis, so the effects of TD at the extremes of age may be more profound.

Bloody diarrhoea is relatively uncommon in travellers, probably occurring in 10–15% of cases.[3] In cases of dysentery, stools are usually of lower volume and may consist almost entirely of blood and mucus. The presence of blood in the stool generally indicates colitis, which can occasionally become fulminant and lead to toxic megacolon. Some infective dysenteries are associated with extra-intestinal manifestations such as arthritis, Reiter's syndrome and even Guillain-Barré syndrome.

In a small proportion of patients (approximately 1%) diarrhoea may persist for several weeks. In this situation, stools may have the features of steatorrhoea and be associated with anorexia and marked weight loss. Further investigation of patients with persistent diarrhoea following foreign travel is important (Chapter 4). Anecdotal evidence suggests that following an episode of TD some individuals go on to develop the typical features of a functional bowel disorder, the so-called post-infective irritable bowel syndrome. This has not been confirmed by careful prospective case-studies, but many clinicians feel that it is a real entity.

What is the cause of travellers' diarrhoea?

Epidemiological studies during the past 20 years have shown that the vast majority of episodes of TD are due to intestinal infection (Table 1).[1-3] Diarrhoea in travellers had previously been variably attributed to overindulgence in local food or wine, 'a change in the water' or possibly 'travellers' nerves' as a result of the stress associated with international travel, but 70–80% of episodes of TD can now be attributed to infective enteropathogens. Enterotoxigenic *Escherichia coli* is the most common cause of TD in all parts of the world, but isolation rates are generally highest in Africa and Central America. *Shigella* spp are also common in these regions, whereas *Campylobacter jejuni* is more common in travellers to Asia. Despite the importance of cholera as a cause of diarrhoea in the

Table 1. Prevalence of microbial enteropathogens in travellers' diarrhoea

Enteropathogen	Reported isolation rates (%)	Estimated prevalence[1] (%)
Bacteria		
ETEC*	20–75	40†
Salmonella spp	0–16	3
Shigella spp	0–30	8
Campylobacter jejuni	1–11	5†
Aeromonas, Plesiomonas sp	1–57	5
Vibrio parahaemolyticus	1–16	1‡
EIEC+	5–7	2
Protozoa		
Giardia lamblia	0–9	2
Entamoeba histolytica	0–9	<1
Cryptosporidium parvum	1–10	1‡
Microsporidium spp, *Cyclospora cayetanensis*	?	?
Helminths		<1
Viruses		
Rotavirus	0–36	10
Norwalk virus family		
Multiple pathogens	9–22	20
No pathogen isolated	15–55	20

*ETEC, enterotoxigenic *Escherichia coli*
+EIEC, enteroinvasive *Escherichia coli*
†seasonal variation
‡marked regional variation

Indian subcontinent and in Central and South America, it rarely affects travellers. Viruses, protozoa and helminths are encountered by travellers, but together they contribute only 10–15% of the causes of TD overall. Certain destinations are renowned for infection with specific enteropathogens, particularly the association of giardiasis in some parts of eastern Europe. Similarly, amoebiasis is not a common cause of TD but constitutes an important infection in areas of the world where it is hyperendemic such as Mexico.

Although rotavirus and enteric adenoviruses are major causes of acute diarrhoea in children, they account for a relatively small proportion of TD cases in adults. However, the Norwalk family of viruses which produces a mild, short-lived diarrhoeal illness, often associated with vomiting, has been responsible for outbreaks in hotels and on cruise ships. This family of viruses produces an extremely high secondary attack rate, probably because spread occurs rapidly by aerosol transmission.

How to avoid travellers' diarrhoea

An obvious way to avoid TD would be not to travel. This is certainly true if travel is avoided to high-risk destinations (50% attack rate) such as Asia, Africa, and South and Central America; intermediate-risk destinations (30% attack rate) include southern Europe, the Caribbean and Russia — although even travelling to Australia, Northern Europe and the USA, regarded as low-risk areas, carries a risk of 4–8%. For the traveller to a high-risk area, the maxim 'boil it, cook it, peel it or forget it' is sound advice with regard to the choice of food or drink.[4] Bottled or boiled water should be drunk in preference to tap or well water, and ice avoided unless prepared from a safe water source and handled hygienically. Addition of ice cubes to alcoholic beverages is also unsafe since enteric bacteria can survive in mixed drinks for many hours.[5] Similarly, food, which appears to have been adequately cooked and is served at a temperature too hot to touch (50°C) may not be sterile since enterotoxigenic *E. coli* (ETEC), *Salmonella* spp and *C. jejuni* are able to survive in food at this temperature.[6] These enteropathogens also remain viable in water, milk and carbonated beverages stored at refrigerator temperature.[7] When bottled water is not available, water purification tablets kill most bacteria, although parasitic cysts can often survive chlorination even when water is pre-filtered before treatment. Boiling for ten minutes is the only way to ensure sterility.

Providing such information to would-be travellers does not always mean that they will or will not be able to heed the advice. A study in Swiss travellers to Kenya and Sri Lanka showed a clear relationship between the number of dietary mistakes and the likelihood of experiencing TD; it also confirmed that only 2% of them were able consistently to adhere to the strict dietary advice given.[4] Business travellers, diplomats and other VIPs may find it extremely difficult to comply with dietary advice because of social and professional pressures.

Travellers need to be warned of a variety of other routes through which the enteropathogens responsible for TD may be acquired, in addition to food and beverages. It is now well recognised that there are 'dangers in taking a dip'.[8] Sea water in many coastal regions around the world is contaminated with sewage and faecal micro-organisms. A recent survey of a beach in the east of England confirmed that diarrhoea and other abdominal symptoms were more common in bathers than in non-bathers, and that the coliform count failed to achieve European Community standards on 12% of the sampling occasions.[9] Inland lakes and rivers are generally not approved for recreational swimming and are not routinely monitored. Recent survey evidence confirms that more than 80% of freshwater locations tested in Britain were contaminated with cyanobacterial toxins; this is thought to be attributable to the increasing use of nitrate and phosphate fertilisers and to unusually warm summers. Up-to-date information on beach and sea water quality can be obtained from the *Heinz Good Beach Guide*.[10] Outbreaks of diarrhoea have been reported to emanate from swimming pools, particularly due to the parasites *Cryptosporidium parvum* and *Giardia lamblia*,[11, 12] almost certainly because the cysts of these parasites survive well in cool, moist conditions.

There is increasing concern about the transmission of sexually transmitted diseases in travellers — particularly HIV. However, intimate sexual contact can transmit any of the bacterial, viral and parasitic enteropathogens (this has been particularly well documented between male homosexuals).

A number of other factors appear to place individuals at added risk of developing TD, knowledge of which may assist avoidance. Mode of travel appears to be important: those staying in five-star hotels are less likely to encounter diarrhoeal disease than the 'adventure traveller' living close to local residents with recurrent exposure to food and water in unhygienic surroundings. Gastric acid has an important role as a microbial barrier to entry into the intestinal tract. Recent evidence suggests that pharmacological inhibition of gastric acid secretion increases susceptibility to *Salmonella* spp and *C. jejuni* infections, suggesting that this may be a potentially modifiable risk factor for travellers. Although no firm advice can be given, it might be appropriate to change from a proton pump inhibitor to an H_2-receptor antagonist during travel in a high-risk area. It might also be reasonable to use a night-time dosing regimen to avoid acid suppression during the day when exposure to enteropathogens is likely to be most frequent. These recommendations need to be validated by prospective studies.

How to prevent travellers' diarrhoea

Despite widely available information for travellers, including the traditional dietary advice and the increasing sophistication of those who travel frequently, there is no convincing evidence of a major decline in the prevalence of TD. Individual studies by highly motivated investigators and well-drilled experimental subjects will certainly demonstrate that such advice can have an impact on the prevalence of diarrhoea, but even scrupulous care does not seem able to provide assured protection. This has resulted in a search for other approaches to preventing TD (Table 2). Chemoprophylaxis has been explored with antibiotics and bismuth subsalicylate. For the future, immunoprophylaxis in the form of enteric vaccines will probably be available towards the end of the decade. Interest continues in the possibility that probiotics such as *Lactobacillus* spp might be an alternative approach.

Chemoprophylaxis

It has been known for more than 30 years that broad spectrum antimicrobial chemotherapeutic agents can reduce the attack rate of TD.[1-3, 13] Drugs shown to be effective in controlled clinical trials include sulphonamides, doxycycline, co-trimoxazole, trimethoprim, erythromycin, mecillinam, bicozamycin and several 4-fluoroquinolone antibiotics. Dosage regimens usually recommend approximately half the usual therapeutic dose. The more recent studies with co-trimoxazole, doxycycline and the fluoroquinolones demonstrate efficacies of 70–90% or higher. The efficacy of antimicrobial chemoprophylaxis is therefore not in doubt, although it is highly controversial whether such an intervention should ever be used.

Table 2. Prevention of travellers' diarrhoea

Approach	Specific measures	Reduction in attack rate (approximate %)
Antimicrobial Chemoprophylaxis*	Sulphonamides	50
	Neomycin	30
	Doxycycline	75
	Co-trimoxazole	60
	4-Fluoroquinolones (eg ciprofloxacin, norfloxacin, ofloxacin)	>85
Non-antibiotic therapy	Bismuth subsalicylate*	60
	Lactobacillus spp	Unknown
	Vaccines	Unknown

*For details of clinical trials see Refs. 1 and 13

Evidence has been put forward to suggest that doxycycline or co-trimoxazole prophylaxis is more cost effective than to treat an established episode of diarrhoea.[1] The most important contributor to the main cost in the analysis, however, is the financial deficit associated with a day of incapacitation due to illness. However, the cost-effectiveness argument is generally considered to be substantially less important than the various risk-benefit considerations: first, antimicrobials may cause adverse effects which are occasionally severe and include diarrhoea. There is considerable reticence to place all travellers at risk of a potentially fatal complication for an illness, which in the majority of cases is mild and self-limiting and which affects, on average, only 30% of travellers to intermediate and high-risk areas. There are also concerns that the more complex a prophylactic regimen, the less the compliance; thus, travellers might neglect malaria chemoprophylaxis if they were also required to take agents against TD. Finally, there is concern that the more widespread use of these antibiotics will lead to increasing drug resistance, and thereby decrease the usefulness of agents that would otherwise be effective in more serious conditions.

The decision whether to offer prophylaxis should be made in each individual case, but there are situations in which antimicrobial chemoprophylaxis may be appropriate:

- a traveller who is making a very short tour (3–5 days) in which loss of even 12–24 hours would seriously interfere with its success;
- a VIP on an official visit who finds it impossible to adhere to strict dietary practices because of official commitments; and
- patients with underlying medical disorders that would make their general health grossly compromised by an acute diarrhoeal illness with the associated dehydration and acidosis.[1,2]

Bismuth subsalicylate is an effective non-antibiotic approach to prevention, with an overall efficacy of approximately 60%.[14] When available only in liquid form, compliance was not easy because a three-week supply of drug would add 5 kg to the traveller's luggage. Tablet formulation is now available, the best results being obtained when two tablets are taken four times daily at meal times and on retiring. Prophylactic action of the drug is thought to be related to an antibacterial effect of the bismuth moiety and possibly an antisecretory effect in the small intestine. There are concerns, however, about bismuth toxicity following long-term ingestion.

Immunoprophylaxis

There are no widely available vaccines yet for acute diarrhoeal diseases. However, the cholera vaccine incorporating the B-subunit combined with dead whole cholera vibrios produces 52% protection against ETEC. Protection is short-lived but would be adequate for short-term travellers. A variety of oral vaccines under development might be useful for travellers. Ultimately, a multivalent vaccine is required covering ETEC, *Salmonella* spp, *Shigella* spp, *Campylobacter jejuni* and possibly the protozoan parasites.

Probiotics

The concept of colonising the gastrointestinal tract with a harmless, but nevertheless protective microflora in the form of *Lactobacillus* spp is an attractive 'natural' approach to the control of enteric infection. A number of lactobacilli strains have been developed which are able to colonise the human gastrointestinal tract. One isolate, *Lactobacillus GG,* has been shown to produce modest protection in TD,[15] but *L. acidophilus* and *L. fermentum* were shown to have no effect in a recent placebo-controlled study in Central America (Katelaris, Salam and Farthing; unpublished observations). Further studies are required to determine whether this approach has any future.

How to treat travellers' diarrhoea

Most attacks of TD do not require a consultation with a medical practitioner, so travellers should be informed about the options for self-therapy (Table 3). These approaches are usually effective for all cases of watery diarrhoea, although medical advice should be sought if dysentery does not resolve promptly and there are other symptoms of concern, such as severe cramping abdominal pain, high fever and general debility.

Oral rehydration therapy

The morbidity of TD relates almost entirely to disturbance of water and electrolyte balance. Formal oral rehydration therapy (ORT) is advised for infants, young children and elderly adults who tolerate loss of water and electrolytes less well than healthy young adults. Travellers with young children should be advised to take pre-packaged oral rehydration salts and to reconstitute these with clean

Table 3. Treatment of travellers' diarrhoea

Treatment	Specific intervention	Impact on illness
Restoration and maintenance of fluid and electrolyte balance	Oral glucose-electrolyte solution	No effect on duration but reduces morbidity and mortality
Antimicrobial chemotherapy*	Co-trimoxazole Bicozamycin Furazolidone Doxycycline Pivmecillinam 4-Fluoroquinolones	Reduces average duration from 4.5 to 1.5 days
Non-antibiotic therapy*	Bismuth subsalicylate Antidiarrhoeal agents	Reduces stool frequency No effect on duration of illness

*For details of clinical trials see Refs. 1 and 13

water. These solutions should ideally be used immediately after preparation, although they can be stored in a refrigerator for up to 24 hours. Therapy should begin at the onset of the attack to avoid dehydration, and be persisted with even if vomiting continues for the first few hours. The newer, lower sodium (30–60 mmol/l) ORT is preferred for children from developed countries, rather than the World Health Organization's 90 mmol/l formulation. Children should be encouraged to eat as soon as possible. For infants with diarrhoea, breast feeding should be continued and supplemented with ORT. For adults with mild to moderate diarrhoea, maintenance of water and electrolyte balance can usually be achieved by increasing intake of fluids, particularly fruit juices and salty soups (sodium and potassium replacement), accompanied by a carbohydrate source (bread, potatoes, rice or pasta) for the promotion of glucose-sodium co-transport. Fasting is unnecessary and should be avoided.

Antidiarrhoeal agents

Many travellers carry a supply of antidiarrhoeal agents such as loperamide as a routine. In an otherwise healthy adult it is entirely reasonable to take such a preparation at the onset of diarrhoea to decrease stool frequency and make long journeys easier. It is not a substitute, however, for maintenance of an adequate fluid intake. These preparations are not advised for infants and young children because of the occasional reports of central nervous system depression and the fear that their use might detract from the vital intervention of ORT. Antidiarrhoeals are not recommended in dysentery. While reducing stool frequency, these agents do not appear to have any effect on associated symptoms such as nausea and abdominal pain. In moderate to severe cases of watery diarrhoea, additional therapy in the form of antimicrobial chemotherapy should be considered.

The standard antidiarrhoeal synthetic opioid drugs exert their effects predominantly via inhibition of intestinal motility. As yet no true antisecretory drugs are available in clinical practice, although preliminary clinical trial evidence suggests that the calmodulin inhibitor, zaldaride maleate, may emerge as a useful agent in TD.[16]

Antimicrobial chemotherapy

In the majority of cases of watery TD infection is mild and self-limiting. Symptoms typically resolve within 3–5 days, and there is usually no real need to provide additional medication. However, in moderate to severe watery diarrhoea and dysentery without severe systemic effects, a short course (3–5 days) of a broad spectrum antibiotic, such as doxycycline, co-trimoxazole or trimethoprim, or of one of the newer 4-fluoroquinolone drugs, such as ciprofloxacin, norfloxacin, ofloxacin or fleroxacin, will substantially reduce the duration and severity of the illness by approximately 50%.[1-3, 13] In the majority of individuals, therefore, the duration of TD is limited to 12–24 hours. Recent studies of single-dose,[17] or one- or two-day treatments have shown that the fluoroquinolone drugs have similar therapeutic benefits without the need for an extended course of treatment. Travellers should be warned of the possible adverse effects of antibiotics such as photosensitivity and other skin rashes, diarrhoea and the rarer, but serious complications such as Stevens-Johnson syndrome. Other concerns about the indiscriminate use of antimicrobials include the emergence of drug resistance. However, self-therapy with an antibiotic should be considered in severe watery diarrhoea (more than six stools per 24 hours) or disability such as confinement to room, and possibly in some individuals with moderate diarrhoea who cannot afford to lose 24 hours from their travel schedule.

Non-antibiotic therapy

Bismuth subsalicylate reduces stool frequency in TD,[14] although its effect is modest compared to antibiotics and it is less effective than loperamide. Bismuth subsalicylate remains an alternative therapy for mild to moderate watery diarrhoea but it is not available in all industrialised countries. Bismuth preparations have the advantage of few adverse effects and avoid the risk of encouraging resistance to antibiotics.

Post-travel management

Patients returning from foreign travel with diarrhoea which has lasted for more than 5–7 days require further investigation (see also Chapter 4). Some of the causes of persistent diarrhoea in travellers are shown in Table 4. All patients should undergo careful stool examination by microscopy and culture, providing samples on at least three separate days. Ideally, sigmoidoscopy and rectal biopsy should be performed to determine whether colitis is present and to obtain histopathological guidance as to its likely aetiology. In patients with dysentery it is advisable to send serum for analysis of antibodies to *Entamoeba histolytica* and *Yersinia enterocolitica*, both of which can cause protracted diarrhoea. In addition, *C. jejuni*, *Plesiomonas shigelloides* and *Aeromonas* spp also cause diarrhoea, often with blood and a consortium of other symptoms including severe abdominal pain. In such cases of persistent diarrhoea, even if a specific enteropathogen is not isolated, a 3–5 day course of a broad spectrum antibiotic may terminate the illness. Foreign travel can also lead to the first appearance of non-specific inflammatory bowel disease such as ulcerative colitis and Crohn's disease.[18]

Persistent diarrhoea without blood, possibly with the features of

Table 4. Causes of persistent diarrhoea in travellers (see also Chapter 4)

Protozoa	*Giardia lamblia*
	Entamoeba histolytica
	Cyclospora cayetanensis
Bacteria	*Salmonella* spp infection*
	Campylobacter jejuni infection*
	Intestinal tuberculosis (rare)
Helminths	*Strongyloides stercoralis*
	Colonic schistosomiasis (rare)
Miscellaneous	Tropical sprue
	Inflammatory bowel disease
	Post-infectious irritable bowel

*Usually acute diarrhoea but may be prolonged.

steatorrhoea, may be due to a variety of organisms, including *G. lamblia, Cryptosporidium parvum, Isospora belli* and the recently identified coccidian, *Cyclospora cayetanensis*[19,20] (see also Chapter 4). These infections can be detected by careful stool microscopy with the use of concentration techniques, special status and possibly fluorescent-labelled antibodies. Additional investigations may be required, including colonoscopic and small intestinal biopsies and microscopic examination of fluid aspirated from the proximal duodenum. Antimicrobial chemotherapy should be given on the basis of the organism detected.

References

1. Farthing MJG, DuPont HL, Guandalini S, Keusch GT, Steffen R. Treatment and prevention of travellers' diarrhoea. *Gastroenterology International* 1992; **5**: 162–75
2. DuPont HL, Ericsson CD. Prevention and treatment of traveler's diarrhea. *New England Journal of Medicine* 1993; **328**: 1821–7
3. Steffen R, Bopparit I. Travellers' diarrhoea. In: *Tropical gastroenterology. Baillière's Clinical Gastroenterology.* London: Baillière Tindall, 1987: 361–76
4. Kozicki M, Steffen R, Schär M. 'Boil it, cook it, peel it or forget it': does this rule prevent travellers' diarrhoea? *International Journal of Epidemiology* 1985; **14**: 169–72
5. Dickens DL, DuPont HL, Johnson PC. Survival of bacterial enteropathogens in the ice of popular drinks. *Journal of the American Medical Association* 1985; **253**: 3141–3
6. Bandres JC, Mathewson JJ, DuPont HL. Heat susceptibility of bacterial enteropathogens. *Archives of Internal Medicine* 1988; **148**: 2261–3
7. Sheth NK, Wisniewski TR, Franson TR. Survival of enteric pathogens in common beverages: an *in vivo* study. *American Journal of Gastroenterology* 1988; **63**: 658–60
8. Walker A. Swimming — the hazards of taking a dip. *British Medical Journal* 1992; **304**: 242–5
9. Balarajan R, Raleigh VS, Yuen P, Wheeler D, *et al.* Health risks associated with bathing in seawater. *British Medical Journal* 1991; **303**: 1444–5
10. Marine Conservation Society. *Heinz Good Beach Guide. A guide to over 500 of Britain's cleanest beaches.* London: Vermilion, 1993
11. Katelaris PH, Farthing MJG. Cryptosporidiosis — an emerging risk to travellers. *Travel Medicine International* 1992; **10**: 10–4
12. Porter JD, Ragazzoni HP, Buchanon JD, Waskin HA, *et al.* Giardia transmission in a swimming pool. *American Journal of Public Health* 1988; **78**: 659–62
13. Farthing MJG. Prevention and treatment of travellers' diarrhoea. *Alimentary Pharmacology and Therapeutics* 1991; **5**: 15–30
14. Steffen R. Worldwide efficacy of bismuth subsalicylate in the treatment of travelers' diarrhea. *Reviews of Infectious Diseases* 1990; **12** (Suppl 1): S80–6

15. Oksanen PJ, Salminen S, Saxelin M, Hämäläinen P, *et al.* Prevention of travellers' diarrhoea by *lactobacillus* GG. *Annals of Medicine* 1990; **22**: 53–6

16. DuPont HL, Ericsson CD, Mathewson JJ, Marani S, *et al.* Zaldaride maleate, an intestinal calmodulin inhibitor, in the therapy of travelers' diarrhea. *Gastroenterology* 1993; **104**: 709–15

17. Salam I, Katelaris P, Leigh-Smith S, Farthing MJG. Randomised trial of single-dose ciprofloxacin for travellers' diarrhoea. *Lancet* 1994; **344**: 1537–9

18 Harries AD, Myers B, Cook GC. Inflammatory bowel disease: a common cause of bloody diarrhoea in visitors to the tropics. *British Medical Journal* 1985; **291**:1686–7

19. Shlim DR, Cohen MT, Eaton M, Rajah R, *et al.* An alga-like organism associated with an outbreak of prolonged diarrhea among foreigners in Nepal. *American Journal of Tropical Medicine and Hygiene* 1991; **45**: 383–9

20. Bendall RP, Lucas S, Moody A, Tovey G, Chiodini PL. Diarrhoea associated with cyanobacterium-like bodies: a new coccidian enteritis of man. *Lancet* 1993; **341**: 590–2

4 | Travel-associated gastroenterological disease

Gordon C Cook
Consultant Physician, Hospital for Tropical Diseases, London

Why travel anyway? Sir Francis Bacon, Baron Verulam of Verulam and Viscount St Alban (1561–1626) considered 'Travel, in the younger sort, is a part of education; in the elder, a part of experience. . .' Samuel Johnson (1709–1784) considered '. . . the grand object of travelling is to see the shores of the Mediterranean'. Many present day travellers set their sights considerably further away than that! Robert Louis Stevenson (1850–1894) wrote, 'To travel hopefully [and I suggest he had acute gastroenterological problems in mind at the time] is a better thing than to arrive,. . .'

A substantial literature has accumulated on travellers' diarrhoea (TD) — a major health hazard to the traveller (see Chapter 3).[1,2] Many studies have sought by means of questionnaires to establish the incidence of TD in travellers to various parts of the tropics. Much has also been written on the best means of prophylaxis (both general measures and chemoprophylaxis) and chemotherapy for this clinical syndrome. However, it should never be forgotten that the bedrock of management rests on oral rehydration.[2] All chemoprophylactic and chemotherapeutic agents[3] possess side-effects, and if antibiotics are used too widely, resistance to these compounds will inevitably supervene. Antiperistaltic agents[2,3] are not without risk, and may in themselves be responsible for persistent gastroenterological symptoms.

In contrast, there are relatively few data about gastroenterological problems (and luminal flora) affecting individuals *after* return to Britain (or another country situated in a temperate location).[4-9] There is also a dearth of information on the cause(s) of on-going (chronic) diarrhoea following return to a temperate country. A study by Gyr and Barz[10] from Switzerland compared the causes of endemic diarrhoea in Bangladesh and in patients with TD acquired in Mexico with those involved in endemic diarrhoea in Switzerland and England. Bacterial and viral causes tended to be a great deal more common in the former (developing) countries than in Europe; furthermore, it proved easier to delineate the causative agent(s) in Bangladesh and Mexico than in Switzerland and England. These authors also provided a 'breakdown' of specific bacteria involved in diarrhoea in travellers returning to Switzerland, TD in Mexico, and endemic diarrhoea in Switzerland and England. *Salmonella* spp, *Campylobacter jejuni*, and *Clostridium difficile* were less common in the developing country settings, while enterotoxigenic *Escherichia coli* (ETEC) and, to a lesser extent, enteroadherent *E coli* (EAEC) were significantly more common. Gyr and Barz also recorded the nature of clinical gastroenterological disease(s) experienced by European tourists. Major problems resulted from *Giardia lamblia* and *Entamoeba histolytica* infection; cholera and typhoid fever were of limited importance numerically, and *Salmonella* spp, *Shigella* spp and intestinal helminths fell in the middle of the league table.[10] Aetiological agents involved in diarrhoeal disease in adult Americans living in Peru have also been documented.[11]

With all travel-related illnesses there are significant differences in incidence between different parts of the tropics and subtropics. *Holiday Which?* has listed the worst and the best scenarios from a health viewpoint;[12] many of the data upon which these conclusions are based relate to gastroenterological problems.[13] It is, of course, essential to categorise *groups* of travellers: the British 'package tourist' is exposed to more disease than the traveller who spends most of his or her holiday in a first-class hotel and its immediate environs. The back-packer is usually exposed to a highly contaminated environment in the rural third world. A further group worthy of special consideration is members of certain ethnic minority groups (especially Asians and Africans) who return to the land of their birth for a short time. It is essential to consider these groups separately: the 'average' British tourist, the back-packer, and the member of a minor ethnic group returning to, for example, India or Nigeria.

Problems affecting the 'average' British tourist

Table 1 summarises some of the relevant problems affecting the 'average' British tourist. *S typhi* infection[14-18] and cholera[19-33] are unusual problems. In *Vibrio cholerae* infection which afflicts the returned traveller only rarely, the enterocyte brush-border remains intact, and the resultant torrential watery diarrhoea has a toxigenic origin. The basis of management must always be rehydration—when possible by the oral route. Typhoid fever occurs sporadically

Table 1. Travel-associated gastrointestinal problems afflicting the 'average' British tourist

---

Small-intestinal
  Self-limiting symptom(s) — travellers' diarrhoea*
  Typhoid/cholera†
  Salmonella spp, *Campylobacter jejuni*, *Shigella* spp
  Small-intestinal helminthic infections†
Colo-rectal
  Irritable bowel syndrome
  Amoebic colitis†
  Inflammatory bowel disease†
  Enterobius vermicularis

---

*A clinical syndrome (see Chapter 3); aetiological agents include bacteria, viruses, and protozoan parasites (*Giardia lamblia* and the coccidia)
†Overall, these are unusual problems in this group of travellers

throughout developing countries, mostly in the tropical zone. *Salmonella* spp, *Campylobacter jejuni* and *Shigella* spp infections are occasionally diagnosed after the traveller has returned to Britain, but these are almost always self-limiting. Helminthic infections are common in tropical and subtropical countries: it has been said that a 'small-intestinal parasitosis is [the] normal [state] for *Homo sapiens*'.[34] Anderson and May have concluded that 'we live in a very wormy world'.[35] However, despite these infections being so common, it is unusual for the average traveller to experience significant symptomatology;[36] worm numbers are generally very low, and the vast majority of infections are therefore totally asymptomatic.

Irritable bowel syndrome

A major problem to afflict the returning average British tourist, however, is irritable bowel syndrome (IBS). Baumgartner *et al*[37] have clearly documented that symptoms associated with this syndrome (diarrhoea, abdominal pain/cramps, bloating, nausea, anorexia and weariness) readily mimic *G. lamblia* and *E. histolytica* infection(s) clinically. Only by excluding these organisms is it possible to arrive at a diagnosis of IBS. (It should be noted that weight loss is not a feature of IBS, whereas it tends to be in these two protozoan infections.) A high proportion of such cases responds satisfactorily to mebeverine ('Colofac') (one tablet 20 minutes before meals three times daily) or peppermint oil ('Colpermin') (1–2 capsules three times daily before meals).

Helminthic infections

A further problem affecting the average British tourist is caused by *Enterobius vermicularis* (threadworm) infection.[38] This small nematode helminth often produces pruritus ani; it is usually eradicated with one of the benzimidazole compounds, for example, mebendazole or albendazole (100 mg and 400 mg as a single dose, respectively). Repeated treatment is sometimes necessary; when present within a family unit, it is essential to treat all members of the family simultaneously.[38]

Problems afflicting the 'back-packer' and the member of an ethnic minority group

Bacterial infections

Table 2 summarises some of the causes of gastroenterological problems to which the 'back-packer' and the member of an ethnic minority group may be subject. Typhoid fever (see above) is a major problem. *Shigella* spp infection also produces a great deal of morbidity; presentation is with bloody diarrhoea, and a life-threatening illness may ensue when the causative organism is *S. dysenteriae-1* or *S. flexneri*.[39-41] These organisms have recently acquired resistance to a wide spectrum of antibiotics[16, 17, 41] The chemotherapeutic agent of choice is currently ciprofloxacin (500-750 mg twice daily for 5–10 days). Although contra-indicated in children on account of its effect on developing cartilage in animal experiments, this agent has now been administered widely to children in India, and significant side-effects have not been recorded.[18]

Table 2. Travel-associated gastrointestinal problems afflicting the 'back-packer' and member of an ethnic minority group

Small-intestinal
    Typhoid
    Salmonella spp, *Campylobacter jejuni*, *Shigella* spp
    Small-intestinal parasites
    HIV enteropathy
Colo-rectal
    Ileo-caecal tuberculosis*
    Amoebic colitis
    Schistosomal colitis

*Largely confined to members of Asian ethnic minority groups

Helminthic infections

Small-intestinal helminths are significantly more common in these groups because individuals are in much more intimate contact with the local (third world) environment. Although hookworm (*Ancylostoma duodenale* and *Necator americanus*) infection occasionally occurs,[1] *Strongyloides stercoralis*[42, 43] is a far more important nematode infection; it has an auto-infection cycle and can remain quiescent for many years — in fact, until the infected individual is immuno-compromised, at which point the 'hyperinfection syndrome' is a serious sequel. Widespread dissemination of larvae occurs through-out the body, usually associated with Gram-negative septicaemia due to enterobacteriaceae. Prominent clinical features of the syndrome are paralytic ileus, severe dyspnoea resulting from larval invasion of pulmonary parenchyma, and meningitis[43] due to either *S. stercoralis* larvae or to enterobacteriaceae. If chemotherapy is not instituted as a matter of urgency, mortality is the likely sequel. Thiabendazole (1.5 g twice daily for 14 days) has traditionally been the favoured anthelmintic; recent evidence indicates that albendazole (400 mg twice daily for 14 days) is equally efficacious.[43] The most effective agent, cambendazole, is not available for human use. *Trichuris trichiura* infections (usually confined to the caecum) generally remain asymptomatic, except in infants and children in whom there is a very heavy infection. *Taenia solium* is the most significant of the cestode infections; it is exceedingly common in developing countries, especially those in southern America, and neurocysticercosis is a sequel.[44, 45] Chemotherapy usually consists of praziquantel (50 mg/kg daily for 15 days), administered under corticosteroid cover (to prevent the cerebro-spinal fluid reaction syndrome), but recent evidence indicates that albendazole is probably equally efficacious.

Protozoan infections

G. lamblia (see above) is the commonest of the gastrointestinal protozoan infections to afflict the unwary traveller.[46–48] The spectrum of disease ranges from TD to severe fatty diarrhoea, malabsorption and weight loss. Treatment is with one of the 5-nitroimidazole compounds, usually metronidazole (2 g daily for three days) or tinidazole (2 g in a single dose).[1] *Cryptosporidium parvum* (better known for its role as an opportunist in the presence of HIV infection) can also produce persisting diarrhoea (see below),[49,50] There is no satisfactory evidence that this organism responds to any known antibiotic or other chemotherapeutic agent (to date over 70 compounds have been tested *in vitro*). *Isospora belli* is a further coccidian parasite which produces both TD and also an on-going infection (see below);[50] co-trimoxazole (480 mg twice daily for 14 days) is the most satisfactory chemotherapeutic agent. Recently, a newly described organism, *Cyclospora cayetanensis*, has been demonstrated in travellers with prolonged diarrhoea in Nepal, southern America and several other parts of the tropics;[51,52] some, but not all, of these infections, also respond to co-trimoxazole. *Blastocystis hominis* has for some time been a rather controversial organism, but there is now no doubt that it can be causatively associated with diarrhoea.[53] Infection usually responds very satisfactorily to one of the 5-nitroimidazole compounds (see above).

Human immunodeficiency virus

HIV enteropathy is a further problem to which back-packers are especially vulnerable (Chapter 5).[54] Members of both sexes continue to indulge in sexual relationships (not infrequently after alcohol consumption) with indigenous individuals in geographical locations (mostly Africa and south-east Asia) where HIV infection is common.

Tuberculosis

Asian members of the ethnic minority groups are particularly prone to ileocaecal tuberculosis. This major clinical problem can present with on-going diarrhoea, weight loss, and/or a palpable mass in the right iliac fossa. Response to anti-tuberculous chemo-therapy is usually rapid, but evidence remains ill-defined regarding the optimal length of treatment to produce lasting cure.

Colo-rectal disease in these groups of travellers is dominated by *E. histolytica* infection (see below).

Diarrhoeal disease which fails to resolve after return

Subacute diarrhoea (TD excluded)

Table 3 summarises some causes of subacute diarrhoea (TD excluded) in the returned traveller. This is an ill-defined entity between self-limiting TD (see chapter 3) and persisting diarrhoea (see below). Small intestinal causes include *S. typhi*,[55] non-typhoidal *Salmonella* spp,[56] *Campylobacter jejuni*[55-58] and *Shigella* spp. infections.

Table 3. Subacute diarrhoea which can afflict the returned traveller (travellers' diarrhoea excluded)

Small-intestinal
   Typhoid
   Salmonella spp, *Campylobacter jejuni*, *Shigella* spp
   Small-intestinal parasites
Colo-rectal
   Shigellosis
   Amoebic colitis
   Irritable bowel syndrome

Small-intestinal parasitoses, especially *G. lamblia,* are also relevant. Of the colo-rectal causes, *Shigella* spp, amoebic colitis and IBS also fall under this heading.

Persisting diarrhoea of small-intestinal origin

Table 4 summarises some small-intestinal causes of diarrhoea which persist for more than 10 days after the traveller returns to Britain. Most infections already reviewed can cause a persisting infection but there is no doubt that the classic entity, tropical sprue (post-infective tropical malabsorption) is better documented than any other.[1, 59–61] A typical example is the following:

> A 35-year-old Australian woman travelled to Nepal where she developed acute watery diarrhoea (6–20 stools daily). During four months she lost 10 kg in weight and felt extremely ill. Fatty diarrhoea ensued. On arrival in London, a jejunal biopsy

Table 4. Small-intestinal causes of persisting diarrhoea (>10 days after return to the UK)

Salmonella spp, *Campylobacter jejuni*, *Shigella* spp
Small-intestinal parasites
HIV enteropathy
Ileocaecal tuberculosis
Post-infective malabsorption (tropical sprue)
Gluten-induced enteropathy*
Hypolactasia

---

*Whilst unusual, this disease, which occasionally becomes overt for the first time during or immediately after tropical exposure, should always be borne in mind, especially when fatty diarrhoea is accompanied by significant weight loss[50] specimen showed villous blunting and a great deal of round-cell infiltration within the lamina propria. Xylose excretion five hours after an oral load was 2.1 mmol/5 h (normal range, 8–16 mmol/5 h), faecal fat excretion, 140 mmol/24 h (range, 11–18 mmol/24 h), B_{12} excretion during the Schilling test, 1.98 g (normal, >10 g), mean corpuscular volume, 105 fl (range, 80–98 fl), red blood cell folate, 202 ng/l (range 150–650 ng/l), and serum B_{12}, 110 pg/ml (range 150–700 pg/ml). Two weeks after initiating tetracycline (250 mg four times daily) plus folic acid (5 mg twice daily) she felt infinitely better and had gained 6 kg in weight.

The geographical distribution of this clinical entity is of interest. Historically, most cases have been reported in south-east Asia, the Indian subcontinent, and Central America. However, in recent years small numbers of cases have been recorded in travellers to the Mediterranean littoral, and sporadic cases in travellers to Lagos (Nigeria), Harare (Zimbabwe), and Durban (South Africa). The aetiology of the syndrome remains to some extent unclear, but there is now no doubt that it has an infective basis. Charles Begg[62] was clearly far ahead of his time when he wrote in 1912:

> That the disease is caused by an invasion of micro-organisms [of the small-intestinal mucosa] was first suggested by me in 1890.

This entity now seems to be far less common than formerly, doubtless because antibiotics are administered early in acute small-intestinal diarrhoea (including TD), and the fully blown clinical entity therefore fails to develop. Two small-intestinal helminthiases, *S. stercoralis* (see above) and *Capillaria philippinensis* [60, 63] also produce long-standing malabsorption and weight loss in the returned traveller; the latter rapidly responds to mebendazole or albendazole (see above).

An important differential diagnosis of tropical sprue is gluten-induced enteropathy (coeliac disease). Although poorly documented, many cases are on record as occurring for the first time in a returned traveller from a tropical/subtropical country. The reason for this — often dramatic — presentation remains unclear, but it is presumably associated with bacterial (and possibly other pathogenic organisms) colonisation of the small-intestinal lumen which in some way triggers onset of the overt syndrome. Hypolactasia is a common sequel to small-intestinal infection of all types. Exclusion of milk (and other lactose-containing products) until brush-border lactase concentration recovers, usually relieves the symptoms (diarrhoea, colic and excessive flatus).

Persisting diarrhoea of colo-rectal origin

Table 5 summarises some colo-rectal causes of persisting diarrhoea (>10 days after return). *E. histolytica* infection[64] is a major cause of colo-rectal disease in travellers;[65–67] geographically, it exists very widely, not only in tropical and subtropical areas but also in temperate countries. Mucosal invasion, followed by colonocyte destruction, leads to extensive ulceration throughout the colo-rectum. This can result in sloughing of extensive areas of mucosa, with the formation of shallow 'punched-out' ulcers.

During the last two decades, a great deal of work has been directed to zymodeme typing of *E. histolytica* utilising several different iso-enzymes. Sergeant, working in London, has always maintained that there are two separate subsets of *E. histolytica* (one pathogenic and invasive, and the other commensal), whereas Mirelman, in Israel, has forcefully maintained that these differences result from environmental factors.[64] Recent work utilising DNA analysis clearly demonstrates Sergeant's hypothesis to be correct;[68] invasive strains are now designated *E. histolytica* and the non-invasive ones, *E. dispar*. Pathogenic strains are far more common in certain geographical locations: the likelihood of invasive disease (involving both colo-rectum and liver) is greater in southern Asia and southern America. Chemotherapy is with one of the 5-nitroimidazole compounds, either metronidazole (800 mg three times daily for 5–10 days or tinidazole 2 g daily for three days) (see above).[1,64] It is essential, however, to follow this with diloxanide furoate (500 mg three times daily for ten days). This agent is a far superior luminal amoebicide and will eradicate *E. histolytica* cysts in up to 80% of cases.[1,64]

Table 5. Colo-rectal causes of persisting diarrhoea (>10 days after return to the UK)

Amoebic colitis
Schistosomal colitis
Irritable bowel syndrome
Inflammatory bowel disease*
Non-specific proctitis
(colo-rectal malignancy)

---

*This clinical entity, which is often confused with infective causes of invasive colo-rectal disease (eg *Shigella* spp or *Entamoeba histolytica* colitis), is under-recognised in travellers who have returned from the tropics.[78, 79] Although most cases of inflammatory bowel disease consist of ulcerative colitis, Crohn's disease is relevant in a minority

A further parasitosis to which the traveller is susceptible is that caused by *Schistosoma* spp.[69-73] Strains affecting the colo-rectum are *S mansoni, S. japonicum, S. intercalatum, S. matthei* and *S. mekongi.* Although it is by no means uncommon for travellers to be infected with one or other of these strains during exposure to infected freshwater in Africa, Asia or southern America, overt clinical symptoms are relatively unusual, a finding that was recently confirmed in patients examined at the Swiss Tropical Institute.[10] Colonoscopic examination occasionally reveals schistosomal polyps, and biopsy specimens contain multiple granulomas surrounding viable or dead eggs of *Schistosoma* spp. Chemotherapy with praziquantel (40–50 mg/kg as a single dose, or in divided doses during one day) is usually straightforward. Oxamniquine is less expensive (and only effective in *S. mansoni* infection), but unfortunately resistance to this compound has now developed in several tropical locations.

Persisting *Shigella* spp infection is an unusual cause of chronic colo-rectal disease. Invasive strains of *E. coli* have recently been implicated in the traveller with on-going dysentery,[74-76] and are probably a particular problem in neonates subjected to tropical exposure.[77]

Inflammatory bowel disease

A further major problem to afflict the traveller, and one that remains under-recognised is inflammatory bowel disease (IBD). In a retrospective study at the Hospital for Tropical Diseases, London, the aetiology of bloody diarrhoea was recorded in a group of British residents who had travelled to a tropical location.[78] *Shigella* spp and pathogenic (invasive) *E. histolytica* were major causes of disease but a greater number of individuals suffered from IBD, the majority caused by ulcerative colitis, with Crohn's disease in a minority of them. A recent report by Schumacher *et al,*[79] working in Sweden, has also indicated that IBD is a major problem in travellers from that country to tropical locations.

The mechanism by which a previously covert disease is revealed by tropical exposure remains obscure. One hypothesis maintains that a bacterial toxin, possibly that produced by ETEC, erodes the colo-rectal mucosal barrier, thus rendering the colonocyte more susceptible to a local environmental insult(s). Unfortunately from a research viewpoint, by the time IBD has been diagnosed, the initiating pathogenic agent has inevitably been eliminated from the lumen. A further problem is that satisfactory follow up of individuals belonging to this peripatetic community is far from straightforward. As a consequence, the clinical course of disease following tropical exposure has not been clearly delineated.

Other colo-rectal diseases which should be considered in the differential diagnosis include non-specific proctitis and, rarely, colorectal malignancy. The latter diagnosis should always be considered, otherwise the odd case — albeit extremely unusual — will be missed with potentially disastrous results.

Conclusions

The traveller is prone to a vast spectrum of gastroenterological diseases. The great majority are relatively trivial and consist of self-limiting TD (Chapter 3), but a minority is of far greater significance. IBS is certainly under-recognised; whether tropical enteropathy[1,59,61] has a major clinical significance remains to be elucidated.

It is essential to specify the identify of the group of travellers under consideration. The average British package tourist is subjected to an environment which is contaminated far less than that experienced by a back-packer or a member of one of the ethnic minority groups in the UK returning to his or her land of birth; the likelihood of serious disease in the latter groups is therefore much higher.

Clinically, it is important to ascertain whether the disease has a small-intestinal or colo-rectal origin. Persisting diarrhoea (>10 days) after return from an overseas journey is relatively unusual. Tropical sprue remains the classic example of a small-intestinal cause, while colonic amoebiasis represents the most florid instance of colo-rectal disease. Although the vast majority of clinical problems relate to on-going infection, usually bacterial, protozoan or helminthic, two major diseases which are occasionally revealed for the first time during tropical travel are gluten-induced enteropathy (coeliac disease)[59–61] and IBD (usually non-specific ulcerative colitis).[78,79] All cases of persistent diarrhoea in the returning traveller must be fully investigated,[80–82] otherwise significant morbidity, and occasional mortality, will ensue.

References

1. Cook GC. *Tropical Gastroenterology.* Oxford: Oxford University Press, 1980; 484
2. Cook GC. Travellers' diarrhoea: slow but steady progress. *Postgraduate Medical Journal* 1993; **69**: 505–8

3. Wilder MH. Counseling the international traveler. Update '93. *Journal of the Florida Medical Association* 1993; **80**: 334–40

4. Gordon ME. Gastrointestinal and other vulnerabilities for geriatric globe-trotters. *Clinics in Geriatric Medicine* 1991; **7**: 321–30

5. Steffen R. Travel medicine — prevention based on epidemiological data. *Transactions of the Royal Society of Tropical Medicine and Hygiene* 1991; **85**: 156–62

6. Jong EC, McMullen R. General advice for the international traveler. *Infectious Disease Clinics of North America* 1992; **6**: 275–89

7. Kelsall BL, Guerrant RL. Evaluation of diarrhea in the returning traveler. *Infectious Disease Clinics of North America* 1992; **6**: 413–25

8. McMenamin J. Illnesses from abroad. *Practitioner* 1992; **236**: 599–602, 605–6

9. Wallace E, Thomas MG, Ellis-Pegler RB. Travel associated illness. *New Zealand Medical Journal* 1992; **105**: 315–6

10. Gyr KE, Barz A. Imported gastrointestinal diseases in industrialised nations. In: *Baillière's Clinical Gastroenterology*. London: Baillière Tindall, 1987; **1** (No. 2): 425–45

11. Pazzaglia G, Escamilla J, Batchelor R. The etiology of diarrhea among American adults living in Peru. *Military Medicine* 1991; **156**: 484–7

12. Holiday Hazards. *Holiday Which?* May 1991: 130–3

13. Elliott H. Feeling washed out on the banks of the Nile. *The Times* 1991; May 7: 1

14. Rag N. Protecting travelers from typhoid fever. *Infection Control and Hospital Epidemiology* 1991; **12**: 168–72

15. Rowe B, Ward LR, Threlfall EJ. Treatment of multiresistant typhoid fever. *Lancet* 1991; **337**: 1422

16. Norrby SR, Wistrom J. Fluoroquinolones and bacterial enteric infections. *International Journal of Medical Microbiology, Virology, Parasitology and Infectious Diseases* 1992; **277**: 273–5

17. Akalin HE. Quinolones in the treatment of acute bacterial diarrhoeal diseases. *Drugs* 1993; **45** (Suppl 3): 114–8

18. Mandal BK. *Salmonella typhi* and other salmonellas. *Gut* 1994; **35**: 726–8

19. Centers for Disease Control. Importation of cholera from Peru. *Journal of the American Medical Association* 1991; **265:** 2659

20. Importation of cholera from Peru. *Morbidity and Mortality Weekly Report* 1991; **40**: 258–9

21. Cholera — New Jersey and Florida. *Morbidity and Mortality Weekly Report* 1991; **40**: 287–9

22. Cholera — New York, 1991. *Morbidity and Mortality Weekly Report* 1991; **40**: 516–8

23. Nettleman MD. Cholera, travel, and infection control. *Infection Control and Hospital Epidemiology* 1991; **12**: 558–62

24. Cholera and international air travel. *Canada Communicable Disease Report* 1992; **18**: 107–8

25. Cholera associated with international travel, 1992 — United States. *Canada Communicable Disease Report* 1992; **18**: 166–8

26. Finelli L, Swerdlow D, Mertz K, Ragazzoni H, Spitalny K. Outbreak of cholera associated with crab brought from an area with epidemic disease. *Journal of Infectious Diseases* 1992; **166**: 1433–5

27. Girouard Y, Gaudreau C, Fréchette G, Lorange-Rodrigues M. Non-01 *Vibrio cholerae* enterocolitis in Quebec tourists returning from the Dominican Republic. *Canada Communicable Disease Report* 1992; **18**: 105–7

28. Cholera associated with an international airline flight, 1992. *Morbidity and Mortality Weekly Report* 1992; **41**: 134–5

29. Cholera associated with international travel, 1992. *Morbidity and Mortality Weekly Report* 1992; **41**: 664–7

30. Cholera and international air travel. *Weekly Epidemiological Record* 1992; **647**: 103–4

31. Abbott SL, Janda JM. Rapid detection of acute cholera in airline passengers by coagglutination assay. *Journal of Infectious Diseases* 1993; **168**: 797–9

32. Ungs TJ. Extent of the effect air travel has had on cases of cholera reported in the United States. *Aviation, Space and Environmental Medicine* 1993; **64**: 84

33. Nalin DR. Cholera and severe toxigenic diarrhoeas. *Gut* 1994; **35**: 145–9

34. Sorvillo F, Ash LR. Parasitic diseases in Karamoja, Uganda. *Lancet* 1982; **i**: 912–3

35. Anderson RM, May RM. Population dynamics of human helminth infections: control by chemotherapy. *Nature* 1982; **297**: 557–63

36. Wittner M, Tanowitz HB. Intestinal parasites in returned travellers. *Medical Clinics of North America* 1992; **76**: 1433–48

37. Baumgartner MW, Gyr K, Zumstein A, Degrémont A. Häufigkeit der Amöbiasis und anderer Darmprotozoosen. *Schweizerische Medizinische Wochenschrift* 1976; **106**: 250–7

38. Cook GC. *Enterobius vermicularis* infection. *Gut* 1994; **35**: 1159–62

39. Litwin CM, Storm AL, Chipowsky S, Ryan KJ. Molecular epidemiology of *Shigella* infections: plasmid profiles, serotype correlation, and restriction endonuclease analysis. *Journal of Clinical Microbiology* 1991; **29**: 104–8

40. Strockbine NA, Parsonnet J, Greene K, Kiehlbauch JA, Wachsmuth IK. Molecular epidemiologic techniques in analysis of epidemic and endemic *Shigella dysenteriae* type 1 strains. *Journal of Infectious Diseases* 1991; **163**: 406–9

41. Acheson DWK, Keusch GT. The shigella paradigm and colitis due to enterohaemorrhagic *Escherichia coli*. *Gut* 1994; **35**: 872–4

42. Cook GC. *Strongyloides stercoralis* and its hyperinfection syndrome: the index of suspicion is still far too low. In: *Parasitic disease in clinical practice*. London, Berlin: Springer-Verlag, 1990: 91–101

43. Grove DI. Strongyloidiasis: a conundrum for gastroenterologists. *Gut* 1994; **35**: 437–40

44. Cook GC. Neurocysticercosis: clinical features and advances in diagnosis and management. In: *Parasitic disease in clinical practice*. London, Berlin: Springer-Verlag, 1990: 191–206

45. Sorvillo FJ, Waterman SH, Richards FO, Schantz PM. Cysticercosis surveillance: locally acquired and travel-related infections and detection of intestinal tapeworm carriers in Los Angeles County. *American Journal of Tropical Medicine and Hygiene* 1992; **47**: 365–71

46. Isaac-Renton JL, Philion JJ. Factors associated with acquiring

giardiasis in British Columbia residents. *Canadian Journal of Public Health* 1992; **83**: 155–8.

47. Mathias RG, Riben PD, Osei WD. Lack of an association between endemic giardiasis and a drinking water source. *Canadian Journal of Public Health* 1992; **83**: 382–4

48. Mitchell P, Graham P, Brieseman MA. Giardiasis in Canterbury: the first nine months reported cases. *New Zealand Medical Journal* 1993; **106**: 350–2

49. Gatti S, Cevini C, Bruno A, Bernuzzi AM, Scaglia M. Cryptosporidiosis in tourists returning from Egypt and the Island of Mauritius. *Clinical Infectious Diseases* 1993; **16**: 3445

50. Cook GC. Persisting diarrhoea and malabsorption. *Gut* 1994; **35**: 582–6

51. Bendall RP, Lucas S, Moody A, Tovey G, Chiodini PL. Diarrhoea associated with cyanobacterium-like bodies: a new coccidian enteritis of man. *Lancet* 1993; **341**: 590–2

52. Hoge CW, Shlim DR, Rajah R, Triplett J, *et al*. Epidemiology of diarrhoeal illness associated with coccidian-like organism among travellers and foreign residents in Nepal. *Lancet* 1993; **341**: 1175–9

53. O'Gorman MA, Orenstein SR, Proujansky R, Wadowsky RM, Kocoskis SA. Prevalance and characteristics of *Blastocystis hominis* infection in children. *Clinical Pediatrics* 1993; **32**: 91–6

54. Wilson ME, von Reyn CF, Fineberg HV. Infections in HIV-infected travelers: risks and prevention. *Annals of Internal Medicine* 1991; **114**: 582–92

55. Cheong YM, Jegathesan M. Imported cases of chloramphenicol resistant *Salmonella typhi*. *Medical Journal of Malaysia* 1992; **47**: 331

56. Reina J. Resistance to fluoroquinolones in *Salmonella* non-*typhi* and *Campylobacter* spp. *Lancet* 1992; **340**: 1035–6

57. Kapperud G, Lassen J, Ostroff SM, Aasen S. Clinical features of sporadic *Campylobacter* infections in Norway. *Scandinavian Journal of Infectious Diseases* 1992; **24**: 741–9

58. Pearson AD, Healing TD. The surveillance and control of *Campylobacter* infection. *CDR Review: Communicable Disease Report* 1992; **2**: R133–9

59. Cook GC. Aetiology and pathogenesis of postinfective tropical malabsorption (tropical sprue). *Lancet* 1984; **i**: 721–3

60. Case records of the Massachusetts General Hospital: weekly clinicopathological exercises. Case 29–1992. A 76-year-old woman with recurrent diarrhea several months after treatment for tropical sprue. *New England Journal of Medicine* 1992; **327**: 182–91

61. Cook GC. The small intestine and its role in chronic diarrheal disease in the tropics. In: Gracey M, ed. *Diarrhea*. Boca Raton: CRC Press, 1991: 127–62

62. Begg C. *Sprue: its diagnosis and treatment*. Bristol: John Wright and Sons Ltd, 1912: 124

63. Chichino G, Bernuzzi AM, Bruno A, Cevini C, *et al*. Intestinal capillariasis *(Capillaria philippinensis)* acquired in Indonesia: a case report. *American Journal of Tropical Medicine and Hygiene* 1992; **47**: 10–2

64. Ravdin JI, ed. Amebiasis: human infection by *Entamoeba histolytica*. New York, London: Churchill Livingstone, 1988: 838

65. de Lalla F, Rinaldi E, Santoro D, Nicolin R, Tramarin A. Outbreak of *Entamoeba histolytica* and *Giardia lamblia* infections in travellers returning from the tropics. *Infection* 1992; **20**: 78–82

66. Garcia-Forcada A, Gascón J, Corachán M. *Entamoeba histolytica* and airline personnel. *Transactions of the Royal Society of Tropical Medicine and Hygiene* 1991; **85**: 700–1

67. Law CLH, Walker J, Qassim MH. Factors associated with the detection of *Entamoeba histolytica* in homosexual men. *International Journal of STD and AIDS* 1991; **2**: 346–50

68. Tannich E, Horstmann RD, Knobloch J, Arnold HH. Genomic DNA differences between pathogenic and nonpathogenic *Entamoeba histolytica*. *Proceedings of the National Academy of Sciences* USA 1989; **86**: 5118–22

69. King CH. Acute and chronic schistosomiasis. *Hospital Practice* 1991; **26** (15 March): 117–30

70. Scott JAG, Davidson RN, Moody AH, Bryceson ADM. Diagnosing multiple parasitic infections: trypanosomiasis, loiasis and schistosomiasis in a single case. *Scandinavian Journal of Infectious Diseases* 1991; **23**: 777–80

71. Corachán M, Ruiz L, Valls ME, Gascon J. Schistosomiasis and the Dogon country (Mali). *American Journal of Tropical Medicine and Hygiene* 1992; **47**: 6–9

72. Blanchard TJ, Milne LM, Pollok R, Cook GC. Early chemotherapy of imported neuroschistosomiasis. *Lancet* 1993; **341**: 959

73. Carmona F, Ruiz L, Campo E. Vulvar lesion in a Spanish traveler to Mali. *International Journal of Gynecology and Obstetrics* 1993; **41**: 94–5

74. Haberberger RL Jr, Mikhail IA, Ismail TF. Enteritis due to multiresistant enteroadherent *Escherichia coli*. *Lancet* 1991; **337**: 235–6

75. Cohen MB, Hawkins JA, Weckbach LS, Staneck JL, *et al.* Colonization by enteroaggregative *Escherichia coli* in travelers with and without diarrhea. *Journal of Clinical Microbiology* 1993; **31**: 351–3

76. Matsushita S, Yamada S, Kai A, Kudoh Y. Invasive strains of *Escherichia coli* belonging to serotype 0121:NM. *Journal of Clinical Microbiology* 1993; **31**: 3034–5

77. Hill SM, Phillips AD, Walker-Smith JA. Enteropathogenic *Escherichia coli* and life threatening chronic diarrhoea. *Gut* 1991; **32**: 154–8

78. Harries AD, Myers B, Cook GC. Inflammatory bowel disease: a common cause of bloody diarrhoea in visitors to the tropics. *British Medical Journal* 1985; **291**: 1686–7

79. Schumacher G, Kollberg B, Ljungh Å. Inflammatory bowel disease presenting as travellers' diarrhoea. *Lancet* 1993; **341**: 241–2

80. Hill DR. Evaluation of the returned traveler. *Yale Journal of Biology and Medicine* 1992; **65**: 343–6

81. Strickland GT. Fever in the returned traveler. *Medical Clinics of North America* 1992; **76**: 1375–92

82. Stark ME, Herrington DA, Hillyer GV, McGill DB. An international traveler with fever, abdominal pain, eosinophilia, and a liver lesion. *Gastroenterology* 1993; **105**: 1900–8

5 | Sexual behaviour of sex-tourists: conclusions from a study of the social and psychological characteristics of German sex-tourists

Dieter Kleiber
Professor and Head of the Department of Health Prevention, Psychological Institute, Free University, Berlin

Martin Wilke
Academic Assistant, Institute for Intercultural Education, Free University, Berlin

Travellers, it appears, take more risks in general, are more open for new contacts and behave both more liberally and more promiscuously on vacation than at home. Therefore, it was natural to take as a background for a study the premise that international sex-tourism could act as a catalyst for the spread of HIV and AIDS. One indicator for this hypothesis is the explosive increase in HIV infection among prostitutes in Thailand. This chapter presents some results of a research project on HIV/AIDS and sex-tourism which the authors have carried out since 1991 with the support of the Federal German Ministry of Health.

The main objectives of the study were to:

- gather data about the social and psychological characteristics of German sex-tourists;
- estimate the epidemiological significance of sex-tourism for the spread of HIV/AIDS; and
- develop recommendations for prevention in this area.

Social and psychological background of German sex-tourists

As an operational definition for the purposes of this study, the term 'sex-tourist' is used to describe a person travelling from an industrialised country to a third world country, who stays there for a limited period (mainly for vacational purposes, but also for business or to attend conferences), and who pays for sex with local women either with money or in kind.

Together with a high 'normal' tourist affinity for the destination country, fundamental to the phenomenon of sex-tourism are:

- a large prevailing difference in the standard of living between the countries of origin and destination (tantamount to exploitation of the third world by the first);
- exploitation of women by men based on this difference; and
- an ever-increasing risk of the spread of HIV and AIDS via the sex-tourist.

The survey

Trained interviewers carried out 766 interviews with male sex-tourists in two phases: December 1991 to March 1992 and December 1992 to April 1993. The interviews, which were carried out face-to-face (by male and female interviewers) using a standard questionnaire, centred on the themes 'vacation, love and sexuality'. Approximately 250 items of information about each interviewee were gathered anonymously about:

- behaviour and motives on vacation;
- self description and personality characteristics;
- attitudes to love and partnership;
- sexuality on vacation and at home;
- attitudes to the risks of infection and use of condoms; and
- general socio-demographic data.

Most of the men approached were quite open, and about half of them were prepared to take part in the interviews. As sex-tourists form a so-called 'hidden population', whose characteristics are by and large unknown, it was not possible to achieve a representative sample. However, to achieve as near as possible 'ecological variety', the interviews were done in different socio-economic settings, locations and destination countries.

Of the 766 men interviewed (661 heterosexual, 105 homosexual), there were:

- 236 interviews in the Dominican Republic;
- 204 in Thailand;
- 136 in Kenya;
- 112 in Brazil; and
- 78 in the Philippines.

These countries are — or, in the case of the Dominican Republic, becoming increasingly — important destinations for both German and international sex-tourism. Although not considered here, it should be noted that the eastern European countries are also now becoming of increasing importance in this respect.

In addition to the standardised questionnaires, descriptions of the locally different prostitution scenes were made by the researchers and some in-depth interviews carried out. Further, there was an attempt to shed light on the supposedly new phenomenon of female sex-tourism, in that first interviews were held with women who had paid for sex with local men whilst on vacation either with money or in kind.

Results of the survey

The sex-tourists were found to be 'quite normal' men aged 19–74 years. A comparison with the total population of the Federal Republic of Germany showed an above average percentage of 20–40 year olds among the heterosexual sex-tourists, whereas the percentage of 40–50 year olds was higher among the homosexual interviewees. The average age of the latter, at 45 years, was ten years older than that of the heterosexuals. A higher than average percentage of the heterosexual sex-tourists came from the less educated groups, whereas more of the homosexual sex-tourists came from the higher than average educated groups.

Marital status

The family situation of the interviewees compared with that of the overall male German population (shown in Fig. 1) provides a basis for the sex-tourist's motives. The percentages both of single and of

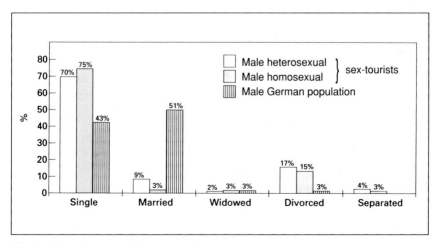

Fig 1. *Marital status of the sex-tourists.*

separated men were significantly higher than would be expected
from the assumption that sex-tourists are 'average' men. In Germany, approximately 43% of men live alone; among the single sex-
tourists it was 70–75%. In addition, only 9% of heterosexual sex-
tourists were married (the corresponding figure for the male
German population is 51%).

To estimate the epidemiological relevance of sex-tourism for the
spread of HIV/AIDS, not only are data concerning the population
of sex-tourists important but also information about their sexual
activity, promiscuity and use of condoms. In interpreting the
results reported below, it is important to bear in mind that sex-
tourists were interviewed after they had been on vacation for a
median of 14 days. Sex-tourists usually take much longer holidays
than the normal German tourist. Their vacations, depending on
the country visited, lasted an average of 37–54 days. The median
durations were significantly shorter, but a percentage of sex-
tourists are long-term travellers.

Sexual activity

Sex-tourists are much more sexually active on vacation than at
home. The heterosexual men interviewed, who responded to this
point in the survey, reported having had sexual intercourse with
local women, on average, 12 times up to the time of the interview. A
minority (12.5%; 79) reported having sexual intercourse only once
up to that time, 38.2% (242) 2–5 times, 18.9% (120) 6–10 times,
and 27.8% (178) 11 or more times prior to being interviewed.

The promiscuity of sex-tourists was surprising in comparison
both with their usual sexual behaviour at home and with average
German promiscuity.

Number of sex-partners

The average number of partners for the heterosexual tourist within the first 24 days of a typical 37-day vacation was stated at the
interview to be four (median, two) (Table 1); for the homosexual
interviewees, it was 30% higher at six (median, three) within the
same period.

Use of condoms

There is apparently under usage of condoms by sex-tourists, except
in the Dominican Republic (Table 2); 30% of the respondents
elsewhere reported *never* having used a condom during their

Table 1. Number of sex-partners

No. of native-born sex-partners	Heterosexuals no.	%*	Homosexuals no.	%*
1	241	36.9	17	18.9
2–4	264	40.4	37	41.1
5 or more	145	22.2	36	40.0

*Percentage of those who responded to this part of the survey

Table 2 . Comparison of condom usage: visitors to Dominican Republic *vs* other countries

	Male heterosexuals	
Condom usage	Dominican Republic (%)*	Excluding Dominican Republic (%)*
Never	9.9	30.9
Incidentally	14.7	24.1
Always	75.4	45.0
Total	n= 203	n = 353

*Percentage of those who responded to the survey

Table 3. Condom usage among homosexual men

	Anal sex			
Condom usage	Active no.	%*	Passive no.	%*
Never	7	17.5	5	18.5
Incidentally	6	15.0	0	
Always	27	67.5	22	81.5
No response	65	–	78	–

*Percentage who responded to the survey

vacation, and 45% were regular condom users. This level of condom use is drastically below that found in a study of clients of prostitutes in Germany, which, in line with the rising trend of previous years, revealed that almost 90% of sexual contacts were 'safe'.

Average condom use was significantly higher among the homosexual men (Table 3).

A comparison of cross-sectional data on condom usage among German sex-tourists reveals an unsatisfactory situation, but there is a positive development in that the percentage of German sex-tourists in Thailand regularly using condoms rose from 29% in 1990 to 50% in 1991–92 (Table 4). In addition, the percentage of those who never used condoms fell from 46% to 31%.

Table 4. Prevalence of condom usage in Thailand

	1990		1991–2	
Condom usage	no.	%*	no.	%*
Never	67	45.6	28	30.8
Incidentally	38	25.9	18	19.7
Always	42	28.6	45	49.5
No response	5	–	8	–

*Percentage who responded to the survey

Table 5. Estimation of prevalence of HIV infections

	Estimated no. new HIV infections*		
Assumed average HIV prevalence among local prostitutes (%)	German sex-tourists per year		
	100,000	200,000	300,000
1	19.3	38.5	57.8
5	96.3	192.5	288.8
10	192.5	384.9	577.5
15	288.6	577.2	865.8
20	384.6	796.2	1,153.9
30	576.5	1,152.9	1,729.4

*See text for parameters used

Magnitude of the problem

It is difficult to quantify the extent of the epidemiological problem resulting from international sex-tourism (Table 5). A point of reference was, however, obtained using a mathematical model incorporating the following parameters:

- estimated average occurence of sexual intercourse for the duration of the vacation;
- rate of condom use;
- promiscuity;
- estimated HIV prevalence among the prostitutes; and
- risk of infection per sexual intercourse with an infected person (1:500).

Assuming that, for example, 5% of all prostitutes in the destination countries are HIV-positive, for an estimated 200,000–300,000 German sex-tourists each year, between 200 and 300 new infections would be expected. This represents about 10% of all estimated new HIV infections per year in Germany. These infected men present a serious danger to women both in the destination countries and at home. It is not possible to estimate from these data the *actual* number of women who would be infected each year, because there are no data on their level of sexuality and/or promiscuity.

In the light of this situation, it is understandable that legal and other steps are being taken in Germany to repress sex-tourism. The success of further preventive programmes is dependent on our knowledge about the reason(s) for the low rates of condom use and how these can be influenced. There is empirical evidence for several possible explanations:

1. More than half the men questioned stayed several days with the same prostitute(s); in contrast a 30–60 minute cycle is usual in Germany.
2. The long contact time led to pair-like, but limited, relationships with the women, who according to the heterosexual men interviewed, were on average 13 years younger than their clients. The age difference between the homosexual sex-tourists and their sex-partners amounted to 24 years. Nineteen heterosexual and eight homosexual sex-tourists stated that they had sex with partners under 16 years old. The extent to which the 'relationship' took on the appearance of a partnership and the more private and less professional the prostitution-setting, the less the likelihood of condom usage.
3. One-fifth of the clients fell in love with a prostitute, and almost 30% of the sex-tourists wanted to return — and many do. At the same time, between 50% and 78% of them had travelled to other sex-tourist destinations in the previous five years, where the majority of them had also paid for sex with local women.

Predictors for condom usage

Using a multiple regression model, it was possible to identify four
important factors which explain 50% of the variance of condom
usage (Figure 2):

1. The frequency of sexual activity and whether the men had
    planned to have sex before starting their journey were
    negatively associated with the rate of condom usage.
2. Those who had explicitly planned their journey for sex made
    significantly less use of condoms. This also applies to the
    particularly active sex-tourists.
3. Less use of condoms was made by married men in comparison
    with single men.
4. An indicator for more frequent use of condoms was when they
    were supplied by the prostitutes.

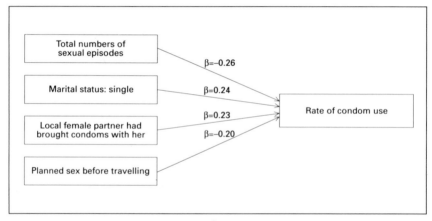

Figure 2. *Predictors of condom usage.* (β = beta values in regression analysis)

In the future, preventive compaigns should attempt to reach the
men involved as well as the women. The success of such compaigns, however, will depend to a greater or lesser degree upon:

*   how well the economic gap (itself an essential factor in sex-
    tourism) is closed;
*   the extent to which the women affected are empowered; and
*   the extent to which awareness by the men of the need for
    prevention and more responsible behaviour is promoted.

Hopefully, future national and multinational projects will
contribute to this.

6 | Accidents and the traveller

Richard J Fairhurst
Director, The Travellers Medical Service;
Consultant in Accident and Emergency Medicine, University College
London Hospitals

It could be argued that accidents involving the traveller are limited to mosquito bites causing malaria (Chapter 2) and contaminated medical devices leading to HIV infection (see Chapter 5). Study of the travel literature may reinforce this view. In *Travellers' Health*, 85 of the 475 pages relate to accidents.[1] However, the situation as reported to the Travellers Medical Service (TMS) is very different.

The TMS provides medical advice and help to people taken ill or injured abroad, paid for by their travel insurance company. The help provided ranges from simple telephoned advice to direct settlement of medical bills and repatriation by air ambulance. The common factor is that the patient, whilst abroad, perceives his or her situation to be serious enough to call a 24-hour centre in the UK for help.

Incidence and type of accident

In this chapter, a breakdown is presented of 7,934 consecutive patients notified to the TMS between 1 June 1993 and 31 May 1994. All the cases were logged on computer (HP 3000 bespoke software, copyright 1992, Green Flag Ltd), classified by illness and age. Table 1 shows the overall breakdown; trauma, with 2,454 cases (30.93% of the total), is by far the largest category, whilst the commonly perceived problem of gastrointestinal disease is represented by 1,148 cases (14.47%) and generalised infections by 686 cases (8.65%). Further analysis of the gastrointestinal disease cases shows that 883 (76.91%) of the total 1,148 are attributable to travellers' diarrhoea (Chapter 3) (Table 2).

Similarly, for generalised infections, there are only 31 cases of tropical infections, six of typhoid and eight of hepatitis (Table 3). However, there are classification errors in the 588 cases listed as 'others', particularly affecting such illnesses as dengue fever.

The system identifies causes of injury (Table 4), which is clearly of great value to insurers. A large number of these cases are due to

Table 1. Diagnosis analysis

Diagnosis	Number	%
Trauma	2,454	30.93
Gastrointestinal	1,148	14.47
Respiratory	909	11.46
Generalised infections	686	8.65
Heart and circulation	648	8.17
Curtailment	555	7.00
Genito-urinary	379	4.78
Skin	377	4.75
Dental	240	3.02
Musculoskeletal	184	2.32
Nervous system	181	2.28
Mental	70	0.88
Blood	44	0.55
Hormonal	31	0.39
Cancers	28	0.35
Total	*7,934*	*100.00*

Table 2. Gastrointestinal diseases

Gastrointestinal disease	Number
Gastroenteritis	613
Diarrhoea	54
Gastrointestinal haemorrhage	22
Gall bladder disease	12
Abdominal obstruction	29
Appendicitis	68
Non-specific abdominal pain	134
Other gastrointestinal disease	216
Total	*1,148*

Percentage of all cases: 14.47

winter sports, which is perceived as particularly dangerous. Indeed, 488 of the cases were due to winter sports (Table 5). Excluding these reduces the trauma cases to 1,966 out of an overall total of 7,446 accidents, a percentage of trauma of 26.40%. Despite this, however, trauma still retains its major position against a corrected figure for gastrointestinal diseases of 15.42%.

Table 3. Generalised infections

Infection	Number
Typhoid fever	6
Hepatitis	8
Chickenpox (varicella)	47
German measles (rubella)	6
Tropical infections	31
Other specific infections	588
Total	*686*

Percentage of all cases: 8.65

Table 4. Trauma

Trauma	Number
RTA* vehicle occupant	158
RTA moped rider	41
RTA pedestrian	36
Water sports	47
Fire at hotel	1
Fire at residence	1
Fall from standing	628
Fall from a height	138
Assaults	35
Winter sports injury	488
Third-party injury	15
Other causes of injury	866
Total	*2,454*

Percentage of all cases: 30.93
*RTA = road traffic accident

Table 5. Trauma (excluding winter sports)

Trauma	Number
Trauma cases	2,454
Winter sports	488
Total excluding winter sports	*1,966*

Percentage of all cases: 30.93
Percentage of all cases, excluding winter sports: 26.40

The age distribution for trauma shows a peak incidence in the 20–29 age group (Fig 1), similar to all cases analysed by age (Fig 2). This is in marked contrast to heart and circulatory diseases (Fig 3) where there is a peak at 60–69 (ignoring 70+ which covers more than one decade), and respiratory diseases (Fig 4) which show two clusters, one in the first three decades and another at 60–69. In fact, further analysis of the original data shows the two clusters have different causes. The lower one is due to upper respiratory tract disease and the upper one to chest infections and obstructive airways disease.

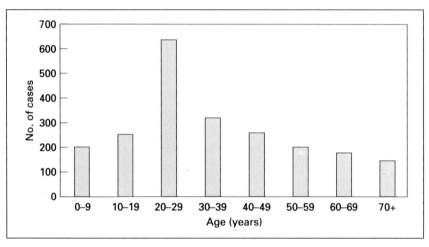

Fig 1. *Trauma analysed by age.*

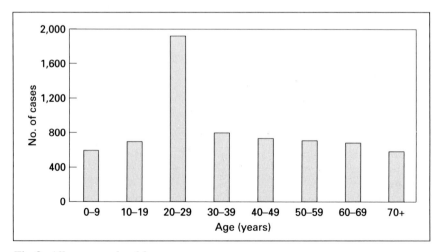

Fig 2. *All cases analysed by age.*

It is salutary to examine the cost of all this illness. It is of major concern to insurance companies, and indeed to travellers who, with few exceptions, do not choose to be ill. Analysis of data gathered in a similar manner, but unfortunately from an earlier time period, is shown in Table 6. The striking feature is that only 15.82% of the patients were over 60 years of age, but they accounted for 30.40% of total costs. It is no surprise to see steep rises in insurance premiums for the elderly, and indeed some companies attempt to exclude them. Pre-existing conditions causing problems on holiday are often a worry, but analysis of the original series shows only 0.35% due to

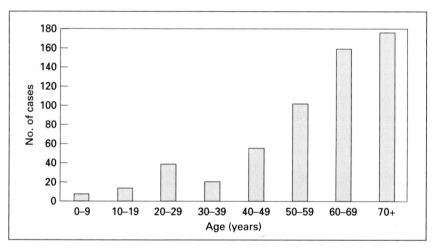

Fig 3. *Heart and circulatory disease analysed by age.*

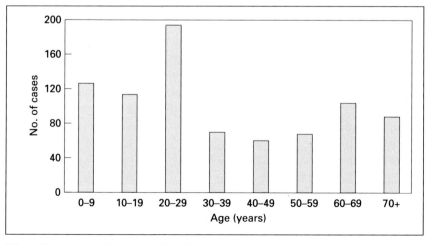

Fig 4. *Respiratory disease analysed by age.*

Table 6. Age/claim value analysis

Age range (years)	Total number of cases	Total value of cases (£)	Average value of cases (£)
0–2	221	122,521	554
3–12	301	124,841	415
13–25	1,384	924,672	668
26–45	1,064	1,247,753	1,713
46–60	558	716,661	1,284
61–65	208	348,458	1,675
66–70	169	404,300	2,392
71+	286	617,041	2,157
Total	*4,191*	*4,506,247*	*1,075*

cancers, 0.39% to hormonal disease, and 0.55% to blood diseases. However, the high incidence of cardiovascular and respiratory diseases often reflects a high recurrence rate of a chronic condition.

Where lies the solution?

It is interesting to reflect on why the large numbers of trauma cases are ignored in pre-travel advice. Perhaps it reflects the too often stated position, best penned by A A Milne in *Winnie the Pooh,* 'Accidents are funny things — they just seem to happen'. In the UK in 1993, 3,814 people died in road traffic accidents, 45,009 people were seriously injured and 257,197 received minor injuries.[2] The number of people killed represents the loads of some 10 wide-bodied aircraft. I suggest that if 10 UK-based wide-bodied aircraft had crashed in 1993 with the loss of all on board, we would have been faced with a major campaign to 'do something'. As it is, these deaths hardly hit the news media.

What can be done? I believe that considerable progress could be made with accident prevention advice, measures to increase the awareness of danger, and risk analysis. Sadly, this militates against the ethos of travel and holiday, which is either to press on regardless or to enjoy yourself free from the cares of everyday life. Unfortunately, those who sell travel, be it airlines, hotels or holiday companies, see preventive advice and action as being counterproductive. No one wants to remind people of reality when they are trying to sell a dream!

The risks analysed

The traveller is exposed to exactly the same risks whilst away as he/she is at home, and indeed the basic strategy must be to apply the same safety standards abroad as in the UK, even if the local laws do not require them. The obvious examples are the wearing of seat belts in cars and safety helmets on motor bikes. As a cause of trauma, the 235 road traffic accidents in our series remain a problem which can, and should, be capable of improvement.

Hotel rooms or flats need checking for risks. Antique electric wiring should be considered dangerous, as should gas or water heating devices and, if in doubt, extra ventilation used.

Personal safety from muggers has been highlighted following the deaths of tourists in Florida, USA. Travellers are always at a disadvantage: they are unfamiliar with the environs, culture and language, and often carry more cash and equipment than the locals. It is a strange phenomenon of travel that people who are afraid to go out at night in British cities will happily stroll unaccompanied in the more dangerous areas of New York or Bangkok. Public transport accidents are common. Although many people are afraid of flying, few take the trouble to look up the published safety data on airlines in *Flight International,* and choose their airline for its safety record rather than its cheap fares.

Passenger ships have a good record on the whole, although ferries have been a problem. The well publicised sinking of the 'Herald of Free Enterprise' in 1987 and other incidents with fire in Scandinavian waters, have resulted in an improvement in primary safety in western ferries. The loss of the Estonia in 1994 with the death of 900 passengers and crew has reopened the safety debate, with attention being placed on bow doors and bulkheads on the vehicle decks. However, in third world countries, ferries are still overcrowded and dangerous.

Trains still give cause for concern, and the accidents at Clapham, Purley and Cannon Street provide uncomfortable reminders of the dangers. In the third world there is the added problem of acute overcrowding, riding on the carriage roof and jumping on and off the train, which should be discouraged.

Recreational risks are a problem. The winter sports risks have already been mentioned. Analysis of these cases shows that the most common injury is soft tissue injury to the lower limb (Table 7). It is ironic to note that an improvement in equipment — the rigid ski boot, is responsible for changing the most common injury from a fracture around the ankle, which is easy to treat, to a ligamentous

Table 7. Winter sports — analysis of injury

Head injuries	19
Facial injuries	4
Spinal cord injuries	7
Spinal fractures	4
Upper limb fractures	51
Upper limb soft tissue injuries	63
Lower limb fractures	79
Lower limb soft tissue injuries	230
Pelvic fractures	3
Hip fractures	2
Chest injuries	13
Abdominal injuries	4
Other injuries	9
Total	*488*

Table 8. Water sports — analysis of injury

Head injuries	7
Facial injuries	4
Spinal cord injuries	1
Spinal fractures	1
Upper limb fractures	4
Upper limb soft tissue injuries	3
Lower limb fractures	4
Lower limb soft tissue injuries	5
Chest injuries	4
Other injuries	14
Total	*47*

injury of the knee, which is expensive and difficult to treat and, at best, will involve 3–6 months of reduced activity. Water sports are the only other significant cause of recreational injury (47 cases) (Table 8). Sub-aqua sport remains a serious concern, not for the true enthusiast who is usually well trained, but for the casual purchaser of a diving experience at the beachside. None of this was helped by the advertising campaign of a tour operator some years ago, which featured a diver in full sub-aqua kit getting on an aircraft at the end of his holiday — a guaranteed way of getting the bends.

I believe that there is a responsibility upon us all to publicise the risk of trauma in travellers, for only the travellers themselves are in a position to adopt a low-risk strategy.

One area in which data such as those presented in this chapter can help is in the collection of trends from injury. In the early 1980s I identified a number of traumatic amputations related to the type of lift without interior doors. As a result, many hotel lifts have now had interior doors fitted or warning notices posted. Reduction of a similar trend of people walking through large unmarked sheets of glass has met with only limited success.

Once injured, many travellers are repatriated for future treatment in the UK (Table 9). However, this is perhaps a smaller number than usually believed. Only 610 (7.69%) of the 7,934 patients were repatriated with a medical escort, and only 140 (1.76%) on an ambulance flight, but all the patients had their treatment monitored, paid for if necessary, with follow-up arrangements in the UK.

Accidents on a major scale

Tourists are involved in major incidents in the same way as anyone else. The organisation of a major incident has special features

Table 9. Repatriations

	No. of cases	%
Repatriated with medical escort	610	7.69
Repatriated by air ambulance	140	1.76
Total	*7,934*	*100.00*

Table 10. Travellers medical service (TMS) disasters

	TMS personal experience
Coach crashes	Italy 1982
	Majorca 1984
	Austria 1985
	France 1987, 1990
	Tunisia 1992
Shipping	'Herald of Free Enterprise' 1987
Infectious Diseases	Kos 1983
(outbreaks in tourists)	Bulgaria 1986
	Mexico 1989
Industrial	Nigeria 1978, 1983
Hotels	Bulgaria 1988

which need consideration. The TMS has unfortunately had to deal with many of these incidents (Table 10) and has a formal major incident plan. Travellers are out of their own cultural and linguistic areas and do not have the facilities of home and friends to fall back on — which compounds their problems. If they are in transit, they may not even have a hotel room. The aim of the management plan is simple. It is to:

- provide the right response (resources), in the right place, at the right time;
- in order to:
  - minimise the human costs in terms of morbidity and mortality;
  - minimise the financial costs, in the short term by the most efficient management of the event and, in the long term, by demonstrating to the public at large, employees and other clients, a caring and efficient organisation; and
  - continue to provide service to other clients not involved.

A recent incident, a coach crash in Tunisia, demonstrates the system well. Fortunately, no one died in the accident, but eight people had injuries requiring stretcher repatriation, and a further 25 had cuts and bruises and a horrific experience on holiday. Within 48 hours of the incident, all the passengers involved were back in the UK. The key to management was the early dispatch by air ambulance of an assessing medical team. This aircraft was then used to repatriate the two most severely injured stretcher patients. The other six stretcher cases and all other passengers were repatriated by tour operators' direct flights. The seats were vacant, but were found only by early aggressive research with all tour operators, combined with a precise knowledge of what facilities were needed.

The ultimate tourist disaster is a major air crash. In 1991 the TMS was asked by British Airways to design and implement a management plan relating to a crash with survivors at a remote location. A theoretical scenario is the starting point to devise such a plan. The scenario chosen postulates an accident involving an aircraft with 400 passengers and crew. Fifty people are killed at impact, 50 have serious injuries, 100 have minor injuries and 200 are uninjured. The injury pattern is smoke inhalation, long bone fractures, internal (chest/abdomen), head and spinal injuries, and burns.

The plan has four phases:

- mobilisation of resources;
- local treatment and evacuation of the non-injured;
- final deportation; and

- debriefing and stress management.

The purpose of presenting the range of possible accidents to travellers, from the simple to the complex, is to remind us that travel advice both to the traveller and also to tour operators, carriers and hoteliers must include advice on accident, safety and risk assessment.

References

1. Dawood RM, ed. *Travellers' health — how to stay healthy abroad.* 3rd ed. Oxford: Oxford University Press, 1992:475
2. Department of Transport. *Road accidents in Great Britain.* London: HMSO, 1993

7 | How best to cope with jet lag

Anthony N Nicholson

Commandant, Royal Air Force School of Aviation Medicine, Farnborough; Consultant Adviser in Aviation Medicine, Royal Air Force

Jet lag is today a most fashionable affliction; it is the 'essential illness'. It is said that film stars get it on Concorde, business-men in Business Class, and academics while constantly in flight between international conferences, but it is believed by many that the most virulent strain is acquired in Economy Class. No successful man or woman can be free of it, and only those who have been similarly afflicted can be sympathetic. It is often confused with *haute cuisine* and *Chateau La Plonk* but, in truth, it is experienced only *after* the flight when the traveller adapts to the new time zone. The quickest cure is to fly back home immediately!

It results from the ability of present day aircraft to cross time zones at almost the same rate as the earth rotates. Journeys between Europe and North America can be completed within a few hours, and a shift of day or night is experienced. After a westward flight, when it is 8 pm in London it is only 3 pm on arrival in New York, and the day will appear to have lengthened. On the other hand, after an eastward flight, when it is 8 am on arrival in London it is only 3 am in New York. The night will appear to have shortened, and several hours of rest will have been lost. Clearly, it is in the interest of the intercontinental traveller to avoid or minimise disturbance of sleep caused by the journey. The most successful approach — provided that the airline schedule permits — is to travel during the day and arrive in time for bed. However, nearly all eastward flights to Europe from North America take place overnight; in these circumstances, sleep loss may be inevitable.

On arrival at the destination, travellers find themselves out of synchrony with the social and time cues of their new environment and, until they adapt, may experience gastrointestinal upsets, loss of appetite, tiredness during the day, followed by poor sleep.[1,2] The severity and precise nature of the symptoms vary with the direction of travel and the number of time zones crossed, and some people react more unfavourably than others. Those complaints relating to impaired alertness during the day are particularly relevant, as they are likely to affect the individual's capacity to function efficiently.

Underlying physiological disturbance(s)

The difficulty with sleep, and possibly impaired alertness, for several days after a transmeridian flight is related to the regular manner in which the functions of the body vary with time. The natural period of body rhythms is greater than 24 hours, but is normally entrained to the 24 hour solar day by external synchronisers or *zeitgebers*; the main ones are light and darkness, though others, such as meals and social activities, also have an influence. The sudden disengagement of these rhythms from those of the environment after a transmeridian flight is the major cause of jet lag.

Symptoms may be worsened, at least initially, by sleep loss during the flight itself and, during the ensuing few days, by the desynchronisation of the sleep and activity pattern from the endogenous rhythm. In general, recovery is hastened by sleeping at the local time so that the sleep and wakefulness pattern reinforces the *zeitgebers* from the new environment. However, it may be difficult to initiate and sustain sleep which is out of phase with the body's timing mechanism, and some individuals experience sleep fragmentation over several days which delays the recovery process.

Even when rest is taken at the normal local time in the new environment, recovery may be particularly slow after an eastward flight. Travellers may take six days to resynchronise after a five-hour eastward transition, but recovery after a five-hour westward flight will be more rapid. It is generally true that the body adapts more readily by lengthening the period of the endogenous rhythm through a phase delay than by shortening it through a phase advance. Indeed, after a sufficiently large eastward transition, readaptation may be achieved by a phase delay rather than a phase advance and, in effect, the body shifts internally in a westward rather than an eastward direction.

The relatively slow adaptation after an eastward flight is believed to be related to the natural period of the circadian rhythm being longer than 24 hours. This may encourage the individual to lengthen his day (as after a westward flight) but lead to difficulty when he needs to shorten his day (as an eastward flight). The time required to recover from a return trip to the UK also depends partly on the length of time spent away from home. A short trip gives the body less time to adapt to the new time zone, and subsequent recovery on return is more rapid.

After a transmeridian flight sleepiness is often experienced at inconvenient times of the day. The individual may have difficulty in falling asleep when it is the local time for rest, and may experience spontaneous awakenings during the night or early awakening in the morning. These difficulties are attributable to the shift of the day or night which occurs after a time zone change: thus, alertness may be impaired during the late afternoon and evening of at least the first day after a flight in a westward direction, and in the morning and early afternoon after travelling eastwards.

After a daytime westward flight it is relatively easy to fall asleep in the new environment as the overnight rest period is delayed compared with the home time zone. Also, the day of the journey itself is lengthened which contributes to a faster onset of sleep on the first night. However, wakefulness during sleep may be increased toward the end of the night because the local time of rising is much later than in the home time zone. Sleep disturbance may be more persistent after an eastward flight. Without sleep during the journey or during the day of arrival, the loss of sleep may overcome any difficulty in falling asleep on the first night in the new location. However, as individuals attempt to sleep earlier in their sleep-wakefulness cycle, it can take longer to fall asleep for many days. Once the effects of sleep loss have been overcome, there may also be an increase in wakefulness and in the number of awakenings for several days.

The immediate effect of a transmeridian flight is determined by any sleep loss during the journey and the delay to the first rest period, the subsequent disturbance being determined largely by the direction of travel. Westward flights, which are mainly daytime, may be followed by wakefulness during the latter part of the night, but probably for no more than a day or two. Eastward flights, however, may lead to more persistent impairment of sleep, and the traveller should at least attempt to sleep during the journey and only *immediately* afterwards, to ensure some degree of tiredness before the first night in the new time zone.

Attempted solutions

Various approaches have been proposed to reduce the impact of these time zone changes. It has been suggested that some strategies may alter the rate of resynchronisation through an action on the underlying circadian rhythms. However, until firm evidence is available, it is more reasonable to assume that most measures simply relieve some of the symptoms of travel and, in this way, facilitate adaptation to the new environment.

The challenge for the intercontinental traveller is to adapt to the new time zone, although the drive for sleep and wakefulness adjusts only slowly to the local pattern of rest and activity.

Bright light

Exposure to the *zeitgebers* of the new environment, particularly daylight, is important. Bright light may encourage circadian rhythms to shift;[3] it is suggested that travellers may even prepare themselves for a time zone change by regulating their exposure to daylight before and during the trip. Similarly, there may be some benefit in adopting the local time(s) for meals on arrival; some individuals find it helpful to adjust their eating pattern (and also rest) during the flight itself in anticipation of the new time zone.

Diet and aromatherapy

Dietary measures have been adopted from time to time,[4] with protein and carbohydrate intake scheduled to enhance the synthesis of neurotransmitters involved in the control of sleep and wakefulness. Protein-rich meals, high in tyrosine, at breakfast and lunch may increase catecholamine levels during the day, while an evening meal high in carbohydrates may provide tryptophan for serotonin synthesis at night.

Aromatherapy is available for the treatment of jet lag, and is sometimes offered to passengers. Combinations of essential oils, used at different times of the day and added to the bath, are reported to improve subjective ratings of sleep quality and wellbeing.

Sleep medication

Sleep medication is an important question for many intercontinental travellers — because the most disturbing effect of jet lag is likely to be the inability to maintain sleep. Medication may be useful for the first night or two after a westward flight and for a few nights after flying eastward. A drug is needed that is likely to sustain sleep without residual effects or 'hangover', and is free of accumulation when used daily.[5] Some individuals also find sleep medication helpful during a long flight, especially when a reclining seat or 'sleeperette' can be used. However, most flights are unlikely to provide a rest period of more than a few hours, and the dose of any medication must reflect the duration of the journey. The lowest dose within the normal therapeutic range is most appropriate.

Melatonin

Although sleep medication may be useful for sleep preservation — at least on arrival in the new time zone — there is no evidence that it has a direct effect on circadian rhythms. There is, however, currently interest in melatonin, a hormone secreted by the pineal gland during the late evening and suppressed by light.[6] Studies have shown that melatonin, given at an appropriate time before sleep, reduces sleep disturbance, and there is some evidence that circadian rhythms may to a limited extent resynchronise more quickly. The usefulness of melatonin and the physiological basis of its action require far more study, and the potential side-effects of regular ingestion of melatonin explored, before its administration can be recommended.

At present, the most useful approach to overcoming the adverse effects of jet lag is to pay careful attention to sleep; in this context, the lowest dose of a short-acting hypnotic can be helpful.

References

1. Nicholson AN. Journeys between continents — sleeping around the world. *Transactions of the Medical Society of London* 1984; **101**: 10–3
2. Nicholson AN, Pascoe RA, Spencer MB, Stone BM, *et al.* Sleep after transmeridian flights. *Lancet* 1986; **ii**: 1205–8
3. Czeisler CA, Allan JS, Strogatz SH, Ronda, JM, *et al.* Bright light resets the human circadian pacemaker independent of the timing of the sleep-wake cycle. *Science* 1986; **233**: 667–71
4. Ehret CF, Scanlon LW. *Overcoming jet lag.* New York: Berkley Brooks, 1983
5. Nicholson AN. Hypnotics: their place in therapeutics. *Drugs* 1986; **31**: 164–76
6. Lewy AJ, Wehr TA, Goodwin FK, Newsome DA, Markey SP. Light suppresses melatonin secretion in humans. *Science* 1980; **210**: 1267–9

8 | Exotic infections and the traveller

William R C Weir
Honorary Senior Lecturer in Infectious Diseases,
Royal Free Hospital School of Medicine and Consultant Physician,
Coppetts Wood Hospital, Muswell Hill, London

The term 'exotic' implies elements both of rarity and of inherent interest.

In this chapter, three exotic diseases are presented:

- leishmaniasis;
- African trypanosomiasis; and
- leprosy.

They have been chosen because of the diagnostic difficulties they can cause, particularly in inexperienced hands, as they may mimic other more common conditions. Appropriate clinical *and* laboratory expertise is required to make the correct diagnosis; furthermore, the consequences of failing to do so can cause considerable — often unnecessary — morbidity and mortality.

Leishmaniasis

The two commonest clinical forms of this condition presenting in the UK are visceral leishmaniasis (VL) ('kala-azar') and cutaneous leishmaniasis (CL) (Table 1). Mucocutaneous disease is mainly confined to rural areas of South America; it is hardly ever imported to the UK. Leishmaniasis is a protozoan infection, with different species of *Leishmania* responsible for its various clinical forms. It is transmitted by the bite of an infected phlebotomine sandfly, of which there are several disease-carrying species; they feed on a variety of warm-blooded animals including domestic pets (eg cats and dogs, rodents and other small mammals). Wild carnivores such as jackals and foxes may also be implicated. These animals act as reservoirs of infection and are usually healthy; likewise, human infection is usually subclinical.[1] In all species the macrophages of the reticulo-endothelial system harbour the organism. In India, the main reservoir is human rather than animal, and blood transfusion is an occasional cause of infection.[1]

Table 1. Laboratory Reports of all *Leishmania* spp notified to the PHLS CDSC, England and Wales. Annual Totals 1975–1993

Year	Total	Laboratory reports Cutaneous	Visceral	Not known/ other*
1975	8	7	1	–
1976	5	3	2	–
1977	7	6	–	1
1978	10	8	2	–
1979	7	4	2	1
1980	13	6	6	1
1981	9	5	2	2
1982	10	5	5	–
1983	14	11	3	–
1984	15	11	3	1#
1985	16	12	4	–
1986	20	9	6	5
1987	6	6	–	–
1988	3	3	–	–
1989	7	6	1	–
1990	20	10	10	–
1991	20	13	7	–
1992	12	7	5	–
1993	9	7	2	–

* all recorded as not known, except #: lymph node histology
(Reproduced by permission of the PHLS Communicable Disease Surveillance Centre)

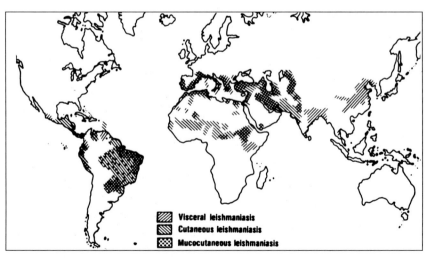

Fig 1. *Worldwide distribution of leishmaniasis[1].*
(Reproduced, with permission, from Chulay JD. Leismaniasis: general principles. In: Strickland GT (ed). *Hunter's Tropical Medicine* (7th edn): WB Saunders Company, Philadelphia 991: 638–42 [Ref 1])

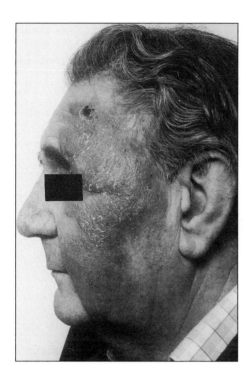

Fig 2. *This man presented to a hospital in 1985, not having travelled outside the UK since demobilisation at the end of World War II during which he had served in the Mediterranean area. His facial lesion was shown to be due to* Leishmania infantum, *probably acquired in Malta during the war. He was also found to have a B cell lymphoma* (reproduced by permission of Dr Anthony Bryceson).

VL is of greater clinical importance; it occurs in many tropical and subtropical areas, including the Mediterranean coastal region of France (Fig 1). There is a clinical spectrum for both VL and CL varying from the subclinical to overt and progressive forms.[1] VL of the latter type usually ends in death unless effective treatment is given. CL usually manifests as an indolent, self-healing ulcer, but progressive types are also recognised and usually occur in patients with co-existent immunosuppression (Fig 2). Both VL and CL may remain latent for months or sometimes years before change in the host's immune status triggers the development of overt disease. HIV infection can result in clinical presentation of VL.[2] CL is also capable of remarkable latency.

The most frequent clinical presentation of VL in the UK is as 'pyrexia of unknown origin' — usually associated with moderate splenomegaly (Fig 3), leucopenia and a markedly raised erythrocyte sedimentation rate. Routine blood cultures remain sterile; special media are required to grow *Leishmania* spp, and bone marrow or splenic aspirate provides the most fertile material for culture.[1] Atypical forms can occur in which splenomegaly may not be present, especially in HIV-infected patients.[2] Weight loss is often present, but many patients have relatively little constitutional disturbance.

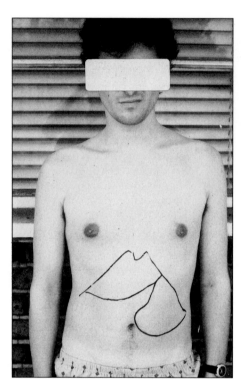

Fig 3. *Italian patient with visceral leishmaniasis; hepatosplenomegaly is present* (reproduced by permission of Dr R N Davidson).

Diagnosis

Some patients may be mistakenly diagnosed as having a lymphoma, and receive totally inappropriate management. Such mistakes can result only from inexperience, both on the ward and in the laboratory. Bone marrow or splenic aspirate constitutes the diagnostic 'gold standard', but must be requested in the first instance. Lack of experience in the laboratory may also result in minimal — but characteristic — appearances going undetected. A DNA probe for *L. donovani* has recently been developed and may facilitate diagnosis for future generations of histopathologists.[3]

Treatment

Pentavalent antimonials have been the effective mainstay of treatment for VL since the 1940s. Unfortunately, widespread resistance to this group of drugs has recently been reported from India.[4] Lipsomal amphotericin B provides a new, elegant and effective solution to the problem: the liposomes containing the drug are taken up by *Leishmania* spp-containing macrophages.[4] Although costly, regimens used for effective treatment with this new technique will

Table 2. Laboratory reports of *Trypanosoma* spp notified to the PHLS CDSC, England and Wales. Annual Totals 1975–1993

Year	Laboratory reports	Year	Laboratory reports
1975	1	1984	–
1976	–	1985	–
1977	–	1986	–
1978	2	1987	1
1979	2	1988	–
1980	2	1989	–
1981	1	1990	1
1982	4	1991	–
1983	4	1992	–
		1993	–

(Reproduced by permission of the PHLS Communicable Disease Surveillance Centre)

dramatically shorten the duration of hospital stay. A standard regimen using an antimonial drug currently requires three weeks of intravenous therapy.[1]

African trypanosomiasis

Despite the occurrence of epidemics of this disease in tropical Africa,[5] trypanosomiasis is a considerable rarity in the UK (Table 2). All cases are imported from endemic areas of Africa, with the exception of the occasional laboratory infection resulting from accidental inoculation. Human disease is caused by *Trypanosoma brucei gambiense* and *T. b. rhodesiense*. The former is endemic in riverine and lakeside areas of west and central Africa, with the reservoir of infection almost exclusively human. The latter is found in parts of eastern and central southern Africa; here, the main reservoir of infection is the bushbuck, a common species of antelope. *T. b. rhodesiense* causes a more acute disease, and is the type more usually seen in travellers — probably because more visitors from Europe visit endemic areas such as the game parks of eastern and southern Africa than visit west and central Africa. Despite these differences, the two species are morphologically identical. The vector is the tsetse fly which has a relatively confined range; the visitor to game parks and other rural areas is at most risk. Unlike malaria, trypanosomiasis is not a disease of urban Africa.

During the bite of an infected tsetse fly, which is usually painful (resembling that of a horse-fly), trypanosomes are inoculated with

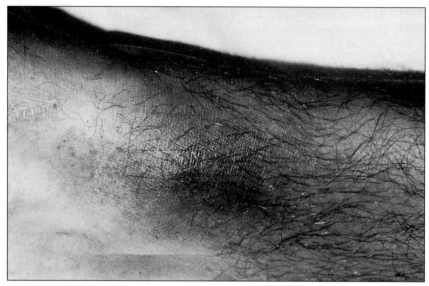

Fig 4. *Typical trypanosomal chancre on the ankle of an Englishman who had visited a Tanzanian game park.*

its saliva, whereupon the site of the bite typically swells to form a trypanosomal 'chancre' (Fig 4). The development of a chancre is not invariable and is much more common in Europeans. It appears as a large boil, but is characteristically painless. After 10–20 days, haematogenous invasion follows, with the development of more generalised symptoms, which may be particularly acute in a *T. b. rhodesiense* infection. These usually comprise fever and occasionally a characteristic maculopapular rash (Fig 5); the spleen is

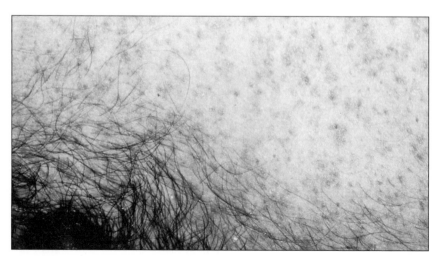

Fig 5. *Rash in the patient shown in Fig 4.*

frequently enlarged, and laboratory investigation may reveal thrombocytopenia with disseminated intravascular coagulation.

Diagnosis

Diagnosis is made by examination of blood films, frequently in pursuit of a diagnosis of malaria when other clinical manifestations of trypanosomiasis are not recognised (Fig 6). The third stage of infection comprises invasion of the central nervous system by trypanosomes; fortunately, most travellers with the disease present well before this serious complication occurs. The symptoms are those of a slowly progressive chronic meningoencephalitis; characteristically, daytime drowsiness associated with night-time restlessness precede the development of coma. Occasionally, the primary and secondary stages of trypanosomiasis are relatively quiescent and the patient presents in the third stage.[5]

Treatment

Treatment of both species is directed at elimination of trypanosomes from blood in the first instance, and from the central nervous system (CNS) if this is also involved. Highly specialised laboratory techniques may be required to determine whether the latter has occurred; microscopy of cerebrospinal fluid may show

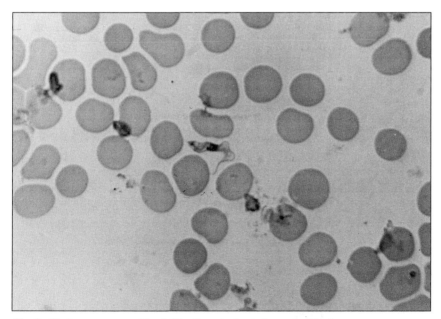

Fig 6. *Trypanosomes on blood film from patient shown in Fig 4.*

Table 3. Number of registered leprosy cases by year of notification
(1951–1992) in England and Wales

Year	Number of cases	Year	Number of cases
1951	46	1972	29
1952	65	1973	38
1953	30	1974	31
1954	28	1975	20
1955	16	1976	24
1956	34	1977	20
1957	28	1978	19
1958	44	1979	24
1959	35	1980	28
1960	37	1981	23
1961	55	1982	26
1962	40	1983	16
1963	39	1984	15
1964	62	1985	15
1965	47	1986	11
1966	55	1987	11
1967	49	1988	12
1968	44	1989	18
1969	31	1990	8
1970	34	1991	11
1971	41	1992	14
		[Not Stated	13]
		Total	1286

(Reproduced by permission of the PHLS Communicable Disease Surveillance
Centre)

characteristically altered plasma cells — the 'Morula cells of Mott'.
Serological techniques are available at specialised centres.

Suramin, a compound in use since the 1920s, remains the
chemotherapeutic agent of choice for the haematological phase of
T. b. rhodesiense infection. The organic arsenical compound melar-
soprol is used when CNS involvement is present. Both compounds
possess considerable toxic potential and should be administered
only by those skilled in their use. In *T. b. gambiense* infection,
eflornithine has recently yielded encouraging results.

Leprosy

'New' cases of leprosy still occur in the UK (Table 3), although
these patients have nearly always acquired the disease in the

country of their childhood. This is therefore more a disease of immigrants to this country than of travellers. The World Health Organization currently estimates that there are about 4.4 million cases worldwide,[4] most of them distributed throughout the 'third world' (Fig 7).[6]

The precise mode of transmission is not fully understood, but aerosols of *Mycobacterium leprae* originating from patients with the lepromatous form of the disease probably play a part, and prolonged social contact seems to be important.[7] It is not therefore a serious hazard for the transient visitor. The incubation period prior to clinical recognition of disease may be very long, sometimes decades.

Diagnosis

Although leprosy is widely perceived as a chronic disease involving skin and nerves, in the UK the diagnosis may often be missed because of its relative rarity. Early manifestations can pass unrecognised or undisclosed (because of the stigma that still surrounds leprosy) by both patient and doctor. The neurological manifestations can be particularly misleading to the inexperienced eye; diagnoses such as 'carpal tunnel syndrome' and 'mononeuritis multiplex' are sometimes made erroneously, with disastrous consequences, if the true nature of the disease remains unrecognised.[8] Various clinical forms reflect a spectrum of immunological reactivity to *M. leprae*, varying with the individual patient.[9]

Lepromatous leprosy — the severest form of the disease — is characterised by non-reactivity of cell-mediated immunity to *M. leprae;* varying degrees of reactivity can be detected in tuberculoid leprosy — which tends to be the mildest and most localised form of the disease.[9] Unexplained skin rashes or nerve palsies in a patient whose childhood was spent in an endemic area should result in a high 'index of suspicion'. Although simple loss of sensation and motor function are the more widely recognised hallmarks of leprosy, other clinical manifestations should also be borne in mind.

The status of the individual leprosy patient may 'shift' up or down the immunological spectrum — towards either the tuberculoid (Type I or reversal reaction) or the lepromatous (Type II reaction) end. Such a shift may have acute and sometimes florid clinical consequences which the inexperienced clinician may not recognise as leprosy. Three cases were described as a 'Lesson of the week' in the *British Medical Journal* in 1991.[8]

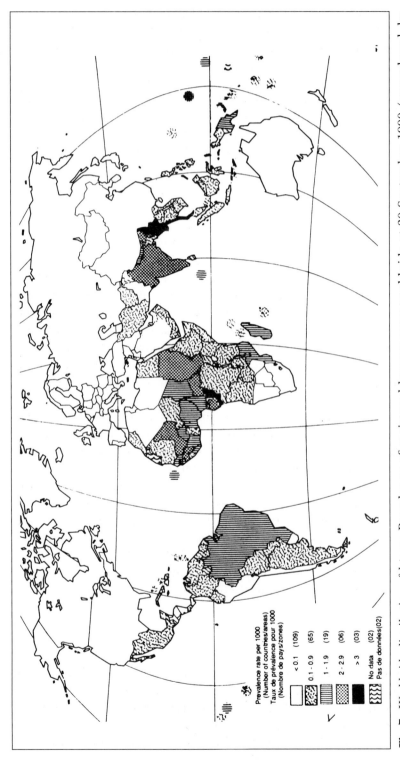

Fig 7. *Worldwide distribution of leprosy.* Prevalence of registered leprosy cases worldwide at 30 September 1990 (reproduced, by permission, from Noordeen SK, Lopez Bravo L, Daumerie D. Global review of multi-drug therapy (MDT) in leprosy. *World Health Statistics Quarterly* 1991; 44 (1): 2, Map 1 [Ref 6])

Type I reactions. Type I reactions are characterised by a heightened cell-mediated response to the presence of *M. leprae* in nerves and/or skin. The result may be an acutely painful neuritis with irreversible damage to the nerve(s) involved. Occasionally, large areas of skin can also be affected, giving rise to an appearance very similar to acute cellulitis — also accompanied by pain. Unless chemotherapeutic intervention is swift, reversal reactions destroy nerves rapidly. Corticosteroids, preferably administered under expert supervision, are usually the treatment of choice.[8]

Type II reactions. Type II reactions present classically with 'erythema nodosum leprosum' (ENL), a term which describes the more obvious clinical feature of the condition. In this situation, the immunological status of the patient has shifted downwards towards the lepromatous end of the spectrum. Fever, erythema nodosum, lymphadenopathy, arthropathy, orchitis, uveitis and glomerulonephritis are well known complications.[8] The potential for diagnostic error is thereby considerable — especially when the erythematous nodes break down and become pustular.[8] Deposition of immune complexes accompanied by vasculitis and infiltration of polymorphs (the Arthus reaction) are thought to underlie the main pathological basis of ENL.[10]

Treatment should be undertaken by an experienced leprologist, frequently in conjunction with another specialist such as an ophthalmologist and/or renal physician because this condition poses a threat to other organs and systems.

In conclusion, the astute clinician should always be aware of the clinical repertoire of leprosy, particularly when a patient from an immigrant community presents with a disease pattern in which the diagnosis is not immediately obvious. Neuropathies and persistent skin rashes where a precise diagnosis has not been made should provoke the greatest suspicion — remembering that a delay in diagnosis may cause considerable and unnecessary morbidity.

Other exotica

Many other infections prevalent in the tropics probably deserve the label 'exotic'. An increasing trade in holidays to remote tropical destinations is likely to expose increasing numbers of unwary travellers. Thus, schistosomiasis may, for example, be acquired on a canoe safari down the Zambesi or from swimming in Lake

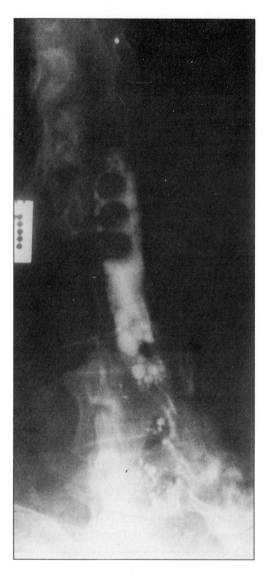

Fig 8. *Myelogram in a paraplegic patient, revealing well defined cysticerci* (reproduced by permission of Dr Guy Baily).

Malawi; cysticercosis may be contracted from package holidays in locations as diverse as Mexico and India. In global terms, cysticercosis is the commonest parasitic infection of the CNS and can cause many neurological syndromes (Fig 8).

Finally, strongyloidiasis deserves a mention. Although more commonly an infection of 'third world' immigrants, this author has seen a number of European patients with *Strongyloides stercoralis* infection acquired on a 'trans-Africa' safari. This infection is usually subclinical and reveals itself only on faecal microscopy during a 'post-tropical check'. It has the potential none the less to cause life-threatening illness if the afflicted individual becomes immunosuppressed, either from drugs or from illness — but, enigmatically, not as a result of HIV infection.[11]

References

1. Chulay JD. Leishmaniasis: general principles. In: Strickland GT (ed). *Hunter's Tropical Medicine* (7th edn): WB Saunders Company, Philadelphia 1991: 638–42
2. Sanz MM, Rubio R, Casillas A, Guijarro C, *et al.* Visceral leishmaniasis in HIV-infected patients. *AIDS* 1991; **5**: 1272–3
3. Howard MK, Ogunkolade W, Bryceson ADM, Davidson RN, *et al.* A DNA probe for human visceral leishmaniasis. *Transactions of the Royal Society of Tropical Medicine and Hygiene* 1992; **86**: 35–6
4. Lockwood DNJ, Pasvol G. Recent advances in tropical medicine. *British Medical Journal* 1994; **308**: 1559–62
5. Manson-Bahr PEC, Bell DR. African trypanosomiasis. In: *Manson's Tropical Diseases* (19th edn). Baillière Tindall, London 1987: 54–73
6. Noordeen SK, Lopez Bravo L, Daumerie D. Global review of multi-drug therapy (MDT) in leprosy. *World Health Statistics Quarterly* 1991; **44**: map 1
7. Bryceson A, Pfaltzgraff RE. Epidemiology. In: *Leprosy* (3rd edn). Churchill Livingstone, Edinburgh 1990: 203–16
8. Malin AS. Waters MFR, Shehade SA, Roberts MM. Leprosy in reaction: a medical emergency. *British Medical Journal* 1991; **302**: 1324–6
9. Bryceson A, Pfaltzgraff RE. Immunology. In: *Leprosy* (3rd edn). Churchill Livingstone, Edinburgh 1990: 93–114
10. Waters MFR, Turk JL, Wemambu SNC. Mechanisms of reactions in leprosy. *International Journal of Leprosy* 1971; **39**: 417–28
11. Lucas SB, Hounnou A, Peacock C, *et al.* The mortality and pathology of HIV infection in a West African City. *AIDS* 1993; **7**: 1569–79

9 | Travel morbidity in ethnic minority travellers

Ronald H Behrens
Consultant Physician, Hospital for Tropical Diseases Travel Clinic, London

This chapter discusses diseases characteristic to, or predominantly associated with, minority ethnic groups and travel. Many of the problems are sensitive because cultural, racial and social factors are involved, including problems in defining the risk groups. Ethnic minority groups are those who are culturally and racially distinct from the natives of the country in which they reside. This definition includes visitors from the tropics to developed countries both in tropical and temperate zones who often suffer from unusual health problems. Refugees and displaced persons are often temporary residents in a host country; their health problems frequently relate to treatment received in their native country or their journey to and/or temporary residence in the host country. Finally, there are immigrants who have settled for ten years or longer and who travel to visit friends and relatives in their country of origin (visiting friends and relatives [VFRs]).

Classification of morbidity can assist in examining aetiology and risk factors, and therefore disease entities. Problems encountered may be divided into infectious and non-infectious morbidity, with further subclasses of diseases as threats to the individual and threats to the community from individual travels. Non-infectious problems include stress, trauma and problems related to the climate and environment.

Malaria

A disease of significant interest to minority groups living in the UK is malaria (Chapter 2). This infection is primarily a problem of the individual and only very rarely affects the community; it is, however, an important and significant cause of morbidity in the ethnic minority groups who travel to malaria-endemic regions. Between 1987 and 1992, 49% of 8,355 cases of malaria in the UK occurred in ethnic minority travellers — VFRs (Fig 1). Immigrants and visitors made up a significant proportion of the remaining cases.

One obvious and relevant risk factor is the low use of prophylaxis in this group. From data provided by the Malaria Reference Laboratory on the reported use of chemoprophylaxis in tourists and VFRs (Fig 2), it is clear that prophylaxis in the latter group is extremely poor, with only 19% reportedly using chemoprophylaxis. Nearly three-quarters of tourists with malaria reported using one or another drug regimen. Failed prophylaxis is therefore undoubtedly another important factor in the increased incidence of malaria in ethnic minority travellers. Unfortunately, there are no data on why compliance is so low, but it may in part be because only a small proportion of ethnic minority groups seek advice prior to travel.[1] The perceived risk of infection in ethnic minority

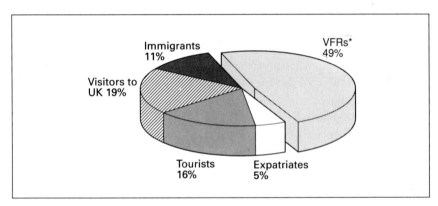

Fig 1. *Cases of imported malaria in the UK 1987–1992 by reason of travel (total = 8,353)* (*VFRs = visiting friends and relations).

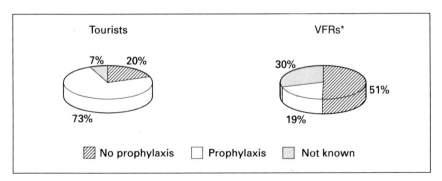

Fig 2. *Percentage of tourists and individuals visiting friends and relatives using chemoprophylaxis* (data from the Malaria Reference Laboratory) (*VFRs = visiting friends and relations).

travellers may also be different: having lived at their destination, they may believe they have immunity, are not at risk of malaria, and therefore do not seek health advice. In fact, the attack rate in VFRs is three times higher than in either business travellers or tourists to west Africa. This may be explained by the different geographical regions visited by these groups, or might be associated with use and compliance of prophylaxis.[2] However, this difference between type of traveller does not occur in east Africa where tourists and VFRs have similar attack rates. The reason is not clear, but one contributory factor may be the lower and more focal pattern of transmission of malaria in east Africa.

A group of special interest is adult travellers who live in malaria-endemic countries and are considered semi-immune, who not infrequently develop an episode of malaria on arrival in the UK. About 19% of malaria patients in the UK are visitors from malaria-endemic countries. A study involving patients admitted to the Hospital for Tropical Diseases in London found that one-third of them lived in malaria-endemic countries. Despite their immune status, their clinical symptoms differed from those in non-immune patients only in time to presentation. Onset of symptoms occurred at a mean of 18 ± 37 days after arrival in the UK, in comparison to non-immune patients whose symptoms started earlier (10 ± 10 days; $p < 0.001$). The presenting symptoms in the semi-immune and non-immune subjects were similar, although the latter had a higher frequency of fever. One-third of non-immune patients also reported diarrhoea as a symptom; this appeared to be correlated with the use of chloroquine and proguanil chemoprophylaxis.

Travel as a cause of malaria?

The pattern of malaria infection in the UK reveals that 49% of cases were VFRs, 11% were immigrants, and 19% visitors to the UK, all of whom are considered as ethnic minority travellers. This percentage of visitors from malaria-endemic countries falling ill when visiting the UK is somewhat surprising. The malaria incidence in west African residents visiting the UK was 0.22–0.40% per visit, which compares to rates of 1.25–1.61% in UK residents visiting west Africa. The symptoms of malaria in foreign visitors appear to be no different to those described in non-immune tourists presenting with infection.

The puzzle is why semi-immune adults who live in malaria-endemic regions and who, as adults, have rarely suffered from malaria, should develop malaria soon after arrival in the UK with surprising frequency. One explanation may be that stress associated with travel alters the parasite-host equilibrium, the parasite escapes immunological control, replicates, and produces clinical malaria. The timing of malaria fits with this hypothesis: 80% of 300 patients studied developed their first symptom within two weeks of arrival. The immunological control of malaria in semi-immune travellers may be tenuous and easily overcome by factors associated with travel. If this is so, the implications for vaccine-induced immunity to the erythrocyte stages of the parasite are significant.

If naturally acquired immunity in adults can be suppressed by stress in travel, vaccine-induced protection may well be inadequate in providing blocking immunity in non-immune travellers with little or no background immunity. Alternative explanations for the increase observed in semi-immune individuals with low parasitaemia may be the effect of temperature in a new climate or reduced oxygen tension associated with flight.

Tuberculosis

An important disease which is increasing in many western countries is tuberculosis (TB). Examination of TB trends in Europe and the USA reveals how travel-acquired infections may infect communities from which travellers originate (Fig 3). Raviglione *et al*[4] described an increased number of TB notifications in Denmark, Norway, Sweden and Switzerland after a previous downward trend (Table 1).

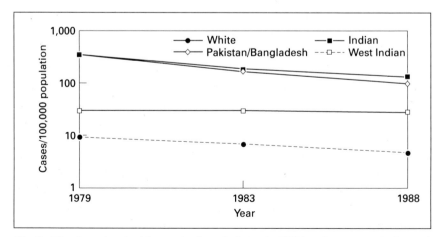

Fig 3. *The changing incidence of tuberculosis in the UK by ethnic group* (adapted from Ref. 4).

Most cases occur in young adults from ethnic minority groups. The authors also record that in many western countries imported TB in the ethnic minority groups, and not HIV-associated infections, forms the basis of increases in TB notifications. The same trend has been described in the USA, with about 64% of the 11,002 TB cases annually reported occurring in young adult ethnic minority groups — with the number of cases continuing to rise.[5]

Table 1. Percentage of national tuberculosis cases in ethnic minority groups

Country	No. of cases in ethnic minority groups (%)	Trend
Switzerland	51	↑
Netherlands	41	↑
Sweden	41	↑
Denmark	38	↑
France	27	?
Norway	23	↑
Germany	20	↑
Italy	16	↑
Spain	6	?

Studies from London and Copenhagen (Fig 4)[6] have linked TB in ethnic minority communities to travel. Travellers visiting friends and relatives (VFRs) in Asia account for 20% of all notifications, with 80% reported within three years of return to the UK. A further third of notified TB cases occur in ethnic minority immigrants, with notification occurring within five years of arrival in the UK (Fig 5).[7] Of the remainder, 25% are probably contacts of TB in travellers. This study indicates that nearly three-quarters of TB cases in ethnic minority groups are in some way linked to recent travel. In Denmark, the association with travel is again reported: ethnic minority children resident in Denmark have a significantly higher incidence of TB, with rates not dissimilar to those seen in their country of origin.[6] The annual rate for tuberculosis in Danish children (five per 100,000 population) is significantly lower than the 68–200 per 100,000 in ethnic minority children. The incidence in the minority groups falls between the Danish rate and the rates seen in their country of origin. One explanation for this difference in prevalence is that visitors from endemic countries import *Mycobacterium tuberculosis* into the expatriate community and maintain transmission at higher rates.

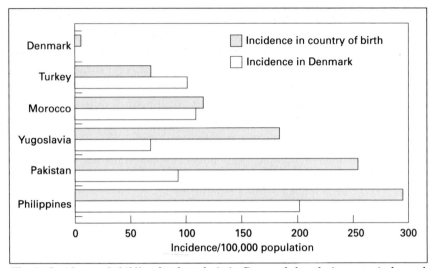

Fig 4. *Incidence of childhood tuberculosis in Denmark by ethnic group* (adapted from Ref. 6).

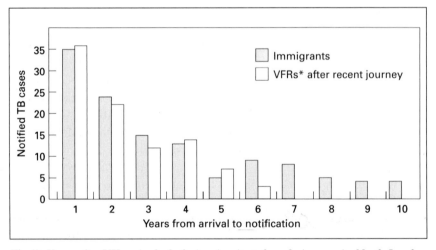

Fig 5. *Years after UK arrival of ethnic minority tuberculosis cases in North London to notification* (adapted from Ref. 7) (*VFRs = visiting friends and relations).

Hepatitis A

Hepatitis A virus (HAV) (Chapter 13) is highly prevalent in most developing countries, especially in the Indian subcontinent where the visitor has a risk of infection about 50 times higher than in Africa, and where 100% of under-fives have been shown to have anti-HAV antibody.[8] There is a potential to initiate outbreaks when index cases return to a susceptible community in the UK, but little evidence exists to support this theoretical risk — despite the fact that Asian travellers return with HAV. In 145 confirmed cases of HAV in Birmingham, 30 had recently visited the Indian sub-continent. Two-thirds of them had received pre-travel advice, but only one had been immunised against HAV. In the 38 outbreaks reported in the UK, none has yet been attributed to an index case from a returned traveller. Although there is an undoubted risk of HAV from travelling, there is presently therefore no evidence of outbreaks related to a risk from ethnic minority travellers.

Sexually-transmitted diseases

Another behaviour-related group of infections consists of sexually-transmitted diseases (Chapter 5); there is overwhelming evidence that disease prevalence in some ethnic communities is significantly higher than in the native population. In a recent anonymous screening programme of outpatient attendees at the Hospital for Tropical Diseases, 51 cases originated from sub-Saharan Africa, and 451 were caucasians from the UK. The sero-prevalence for HIV was 33.2% in the sub-Saharan native travellers and 1.8% in the caucasians.[9] These data must be interpreted with caution because screening in the majority of the UK subjects, most of whom were asymptomatic, was undertaken as part of a post-tropical check-up, while many of the ethnic minority travellers had presented because of symptoms possibly related to their underlying infection.

Refugees and travel

Refugees are particularly susceptible to outbreaks of infectious diseases. Temporary residences tend to be associated with inadequate health services, poor sanitation and food, making the refugees more susceptible to infectious agents. Introduction of pathogens to this group often has devastating results. One such example was an outbreak of multidrug-resistant *Shigella dysenteriae* type 1 in eastern Transvaal in a refugee camp.[10] The outbreak involved 34 adult patients who presented with a haemolytic syndrome causing a severe disease. The organism responsible probably originated in Mozambique and was imported by an influx of refugees. A second example was the massive outbreak of cholera and dysentery in Rwandan refugee camps on the Zaire border in 1994.

Conclusion

The epidemiology, susceptibility and presentation of both infectious and non-infectious problems in ethnic minority groups in the UK may differ from patterns present in the native population. Travel is one of the more important factors in these differences, particularly the *reason* for travel — refugees and individuals travelling to tropical countries are at special risk. Many of the problems are related to social, cultural and economic factors, and tackling them is frequently difficult. Trends and patterns of disease, although often recognised, are not always a priority for the host nation, especially when the problems do not affect the majority of the population.

References

1. Genton B, Behrens RH. Specialised travel consultation. Part 2: Acquiring knowledge. *Journal of Travel Medicine* 1994; **1**: 13–5
2. Phillips-Howard PA, Porter J, Behrens RH, Bradley DJ. Epidemic alert: malaria infections in travellers from West Africa. *Lancet* 1990; **335**: 119–20
3. Davies PDO. Tuberculosis in immigrants, ethnic minorities and the homeless. In: Davies PDO, ed. *Clinical Tuberculosis*. London: Chapman and Hall, 1994: 191–207
4. Raviglione MC, Sudre P, Rieder HL, Spinaci S, Kochi A. Secular trends of tuberculosis in Western Europe. *Bulletin of the World Health Organization* 1993; **71**: 297–306
5. Bloch AB, Rieder HL, Kelly GD, Cauthen GM, *et al*. The epidemiology of tuberculosis in the United States. Implications for diagnosis and treatment. *Clinics in Chest Medicine* 1989; **10**: 297–313
6. Mortensen J, Lange P, Storm HK, Viskum K. Childhood tuberculosis in a developed country. *European Respiratory Journal* 1989; **2**: 985–7
7. McCarthy OR. Asian immigrant tuberculosis — the effect of visiting Asia. *British Journal of Diseases of the Chest* 1984; **78**: 248–53
8. Jilg W. Adult use of hepatitis A vaccine in developed countries. *Vaccine* 1993; **11** (Suppl 1): S6–8
9. Hawks SJ, Malin AS, Araru T, Mabey D. HIV infection among heterosexual travellers attending the Hospital for Tropical Diseases, London. *Genitourinary Medicine* 1992; **68**: 309–11
10. Bloom PD, MacPhail AC, Klugman K, Louw M, *et al*. Haemolytic-uraemic syndrome in adults with resistant *Shigella dysenteriae* type 1. *Lancet* 1994; **344**: 206

10 | Issues for long-term and expatriate travellers

David R Hill
Division of Infectious Diseases, University of Connecticut Health Center, Farmington, CT, USA

Long-term and expatriate travellers are at risk for both infectious and non-infectious illness through their prolonged residence overseas. This chapter will highlight the important aspects of health care for this group, and discuss them in terms of preparation before travel, health events that occur during travel, and the evaluation of the returned traveller.

Who are long-term and expatriate travellers, and what constitutes long-term travel? Study of travel epidemiology indicates that the median duration of travel to the developing world is 21 days; two-thirds travel for one month or less, and only 6% are away for a year or more (Table 1).[1] Passenger surveys of individuals travelling from the UK to Kenya, a country visited annually by more than 115,000 UK residents in recent years, confirms this typically short duration of travel: the average duration in 1992 was 22 days.

Table 1. Characteristics of long-term travellers*

	Duration of travel		
	< 30 days	≥ 30 days	≥ 1 year
Travellers (%)	67	33	6
Mean age (years)	46.9	33.1	27.1
Sex (% female)	54	55	54
Purpose (%)			
pleasure	79	46	20
business	10	15	44
study/teaching	7	31	17
missionary	4	8	20

*Information for 3,863 travellers from the International Traveler's Medical Service, University of Connecticut Health Center, Farmington, USA, January 1984 to June 1992

Therefore, most pre-travel advice is targeted toward the short-term traveller (≤ one month). Based on this information, individuals going for more than one month may be categorised as long-term travellers; however, others would confine the term to those travelling for six months or more.

What else is known about these travellers? They are younger, more frequently travelling with dependents, and going for business, study or teaching programmes, and missionary activities more than for pleasure (Table 1). Within the category is the expatriate traveller. It is important to distinguish expatriates since they constitute a separate group in terms of health risk(s) and access to care while overseas. Expatriates often differ from other long-term travellers because they have been sent by the Foreign and Commonwealth Office, a multinational corporation or by private organisations, concerned with voluntary aid, research, medical or missionary activities. These organisations usually have experience of working in the country, and have established contacts with the national community at multiple levels. The expatriate often lives in a single area, which may be rural or urban, and is frequently accompanied by family or is planning to have children.[2] There may also be an expatriate community with an existing support network including physicians.

Other long-term travellers may be less settled. They are frequently young, travelling overland through multiple countries with no specific base. Their duration of travel, broad itinerary and rural exposure means that they become exposed to vectors of a broad range of infections. It is also likely that younger travellers will be less careful in many areas such as personal safety and sexual activity, and less compliant with medical advice, therefore placing themselves at higher risk for illness and accident while overseas.[3–5] They may not have established contacts in the countries in which they are travelling, and if they become ill find it more difficult to locate and obtain medical care.

Pre-travel preparations (see also Chapter 11)

Medical advice

The preparation of long-term travellers will be more comprehensive than that of short-term travellers. In addition to providing the standard immunisations and antimalarial tablets, there needs to be advice about the issues of living overseas. As with all travellers, it is important to determine the *actual* health risk during travel by taking into account their health status and itinerary, not only in the country visited but also the areas within each country. A banking executive sent to Nairobi will have far less disease exposure than a medical researcher performing malaria investigations on the shores of Lake Victoria, for example.

Pre-travel medical screening may be performed by a physician in travel medicine, although this task will more frequently fall upon the sponsoring organisation, a general physician, or a physician in occupational medicine. Travel medicine physicians should, however, be able to recognise major problems which would contra-indicate travel — for example, unstable angina, severe chronic obstructive pulmonary disease and poorly compensated psychiatric illness. As part of medical screening, it is necessary to assess the effect(s) of climate or altitude upon any underlying medical conditions.[6] Long-term travellers should be able to work under environmental conditions which may be both physically and mentally demanding. The goal is to ensure that they go on their journey healthy and fit; while overseas, they should adhere to practices which will maintain this.

Some countries may require HIV testing before granting a work or temporary residence visa. If mandatory, the physician will need to discuss the implications of the test. A traveller who is HIV-positive should think carefully about overseas work because of the exposure to many deleterious pathogens and the potentially limited access to a required level of health care should he/she become ill.[7, 8] All long-term travellers should be screened for tuberculosis infection prior to travel and know their blood group.

Long-term travellers should be fully immunised.[9] When the benefit of various vaccines is discussed, it is usually based on the risks of persons travelling for three weeks or less. Those who remain overseas for months or years, however, will necessarily have an increased cumulative risk. Errors in food and liquid hygiene, travel to remote destinations, and failure to comply with antimalarial prophylaxis are all more likely to occur over months or years.

Immunisations. Several immunisations are important to highlight for long-term travellers (Table 2). Travellers should be up-to-date on routinely recommended immunisations. If they were born after 1957, this would include a booster against measles — an illness with considerably higher risk overseas.[10] Recent outbreaks of diphtheria in inadequately protected populations indicate that this should be included along with tetanus boosting.[11] The immunisations recommended because of disease exposure, include protection against both hepatitis A (HAV) and B (HBV) (see Chapter 13). In some

Table 2. Immunisations for travellers*

Routine	Required	Recommended
Tetanus	Yellow fever	Hepatitis A
Diphtheria	Cholera**	Hepatitis B
Measles		Typhoid
Polio		Meningococcus
Influenza		Rabies
Pneumococcus		Japanese encephalitis

*Immunisations may be routinely recommended for health maintenance-based on age- or health-appropriate standards, required for entry into a country, or recommended because of exposure during travel.
**Cholera immunisation is no longer required for travel; however, some countries may still ask for evidence of vaccination.

travellers, it is appropriate to check IgG anti-HAV antibodies to avoid repeated injections of either immunoglobulin or inactivated vaccine. Studies have demonstrated that individuals aged 50 or older, who were born or have had prolonged residence in a developing country or a history of jaundice, have a high chance of being immune to HAV.[12] People who will be residing in or travelling to endemic areas should be protected against rabies, Japanese encephalitis and meningococcal infection. In addition to vaccination, appropriate preventive advice on these diseases should be conveyed, preferably in written form.

Malaria prevention. Another critical area about which the traveller should be informed is malaria prevention (Chapter 2). Prevention requires both avoidance of mosquito bites and safe and effective antimalarial medications. It is assumed that travellers will be at continuous exposure to malaria, and thus at continuous risk, so they should comply with preventive measures throughout their stay in the tropics. Mosquito avoidance includes the screening of homes, the use of pyrethrum impregnated bed-nets, the consistent application of repellents, and the wearing of clothing which reduces the likelihood of bites.[13] By themselves, these measures will go a long way to decreasing the risk of malaria.[14] Diethyl-methyl-toluamide (DEET) — containing products appear to be the most effective repellents. They do not need to be highly concentrated, and should be applied sparingly to small children since toxic neurological reactions have been described when highly concentrated preparations are applied liberally.[15]

Are antimalarials safe for years of continuous use? Will the traveller be consistent in taking them — sometimes daily, for this length of time? The major antimalarials recommended by UK physicians are chloroquine, proguanil, mefloquine, and occasionally doxycycline (see Chapter 2).[16] The first problem arises in prescribing these drugs for months to years. There is no limit to the duration of chloroquine and proguanil use, but mefloquine should be restricted to one year (D J Bradley, personal communication). What does the traveller do when this period is up? Should the drug be stopped for a while and then restarted, should it be continued despite the recommendations, or should there be a change to another antimalarial? These issues are not resolved, but it should be noted that the USA and several European countries have not placed time limits on the duration of mefloquine use.[13,17]

Are antimalarials safe for the long-term traveller? In general, they are very safe, and concern about safety should not be a reason for discontinuation (Table 3). Chloroquine has been taken safely for more than 40 years in doses used for malaria prophylaxis. It can cause mild gastrointestinal side-effects and pruritus, especially in Africans. Retinal toxicity with chloroquine is well described, but this has been limited to people taking daily chloroquine for rheumatic disorders.[18] Two thresholds for the risk of retinopathy have been described:

- a total cumulative dose of 100 g of chloroquine base; and
- a daily dose of 250 mg (4 mg/kg).[18]

Using the first threshold, an adult would have to take continuous weekly chloroquine for about six years. However, data suggest that the daily dose is a more accurate predictor of toxicity; very

Table 3. Toxicity of antimalarials

	Side-effects	
Antimalarial	Minor	Major
Chloroquine	GI*, pruritus, Worsening of psoriasis, Hair loss	[Retinopathy]
Proguanil	GI, Mouth ulcers	
Mefloquine	GI, Headache, Dizziness, Concentration defects	Neuropsychiatric, Cardiac
Doxycycline	GI, Photosensitivity, Vaginal yeast infections	Bone/teeth deposits in children < 8 years

*GI = gastrointestinal

high cumulative amounts have been taken without sequelae. This daily dose should not exceed 3.5–4 mg/kg.[18-20] Therefore, travellers would not be at risk for toxicity, and the statement can be made that retinopathy has rarely, if ever, been reported in patients taking weekly prophylactic doses.[18] If travellers are concerned, they can undergo an ophthalmological examination on a six-month to yearly basis after several years of use.

Proguanil is well tolerated, and has no serious side-effects. Gastrointestinal disturbance and aphthous mouth ulcers occur in up to 25% of users and may be more frequent in those on combined chloroquine/proguanil.[18, 21, 22]

Concern has been raised about the toxicity of mefloquine; however, multiple studies have now demonstrated that when taken in prophylactic dosages (250 mg/week) it is well tolerated and comparable to other regimens.[23-25] Severe neuropsychiatric effects appear to be most pronounced after high-dose therapeutic use, but may occur in only one out of 10,000–15,000 prophylactic users.[26,27] Cardiac toxicity is probably overemphasised, but concurrent use with halofantrine and quinine should be avoided.[17,25] There is little information on the use of this compound beyond two years, but no evidence of cumulative toxicity.[23,28] Doxycycline may cause photosensitivity, predispose to vaginal yeast infections, and should not be used in children less than eight years old.[17,18]

Compliance is the other important issue in malaria prevention. Data from short-term travellers indicate that complete compliance with correct medication occurs in only 42–64% of travellers.[29-32] Compliance decreases with longer duration of travel.[32,33] Reasons cited for failure to take antimalarials are fear of long-term side-effects, conflicting or complicated medical advice on either the correct medication or whether medications are needed at all, and the perception that the medications are not working.[29,31,33] During the pre-travel visit to the physician, the importance of continuous antimalarial measures, including chemoprophylaxis, should be emphasised in a consistent and straightforward manner. Preferably only one regimen should be recommended.[31] If this can be accomplished, compliance of over 80% may be achieved.[34]

Diarrhoeal disease prevention. Diarrhoea prevention has been covered in other sections (Chapters 3 and 4); however, several issues are pertinent to the long-term traveller. First, prophylactic antibiotics are not a consideration, since there is no information on their use for more than three weeks.[35] Instead, careful instructions should be given about the safe preparation of food and liquids, and the administration of prompt therapy when diarrhoea occurs. The mainstay of therapy is rehydration; in selective circumstances, anti-motility agents and antimicrobials may be used.[35]

Although there are many other risk factors for the long-term traveller, it is not always possible to discuss all of them during the pre-travel visit. Precautions against vector-borne diseases such as schistosomiasis, onchocerciasis and leishmaniasis (Chapter 8), and behavioural avoidance of sexually transmitted diseases (Chapter 5), are for example important issues for the traveller. If there is sufficient time, these can be raised in the pre-travel visit or information provided in written form. Hopefully, the sponsoring agency for expatriates will have taken the trouble to develop a detailed programme to prepare its employees for overseas work. All travellers, however, should be instructed that if any of the major clinical symptoms occur, medical care should be sought promptly — for example, prolonged or high fever, persistent rash, malabsorption with weight loss, and neurological symptoms.

Access to medical care

How is medical care located overseas? The provision of health care is a critical issue for the long-term traveller since it is likely that this will be required at some time. In a study of Swedish expatriates, 85% reported some health impairment and 15% were admitted to hospital.[36] Obtaining care will be more difficult for the overland traveller than for the expatriate since it is likely that the latter will have access to either a national or an expatriate physician within his or her working community.

If medical care is obtained, what about its quality? A study of American travellers who sought medical care from national sources for diarrhoeal illness indicated that only 50% of them felt that the treatment received was beneficial.[34] Medical care in the developing world is also frequently associated with the use of injections, raising the potential for transmission of blood-borne pathogens such as HBV, HCV and HIV.

If possible, travellers should be provided with the names and locations of physicians, health care facilities or points of information. A query in the embassy or consulate will be helpful in obtaining referrals. Mission hospitals are also excellent centres. Major hotels will have physicians on call, but the quality may be variable. Some organisations and publications will provide information about local health care. One such organisation, the International Association for Medical Assistance to Travelers (IAMAT) (417 Center St, Lewiston, NY 14092, USA), provides the names and addresses of English-speaking physicians throughout the world. Finally, travellers should also be aware that cash payment for medical care may be required.

In order to deal with both aspects of this problem — assistance in obtaining medical care and payment of bills — long-term travellers should purchase a travel insurance policy.[37–39] Helpful aspects of these policies are listed in Table 4. They should provide not only reimbursement or cash payment of medical bills but also assistance in locating and evaluating medical care. Air evacuation or repatriation may be necessary — depending upon the traveller's medical conditon and the quality of local health care. Some policies will assist both in assessing the medical situation and in arranging for evacuation. Other helpful features of the policy cover trip interruption and baggage loss.

Cultural adaptation

The selection and preparation of personnel for an overseas assignment are critical to the success of any organisation. Many a foreign posting has been abandoned because the stresses of cultural adaptation have been too great and have led to family disruption, depression or alcohol dependence.[40] It is not the role of the travel medicine physician to perform psychological screening and cultural training, but it is helpful to review the challenges to the long-term and expatriate traveller (Table 5).[40] Personal qualities that may lead to a successful overseas 'experience' include enthusiasm, a positive outlook, self assurance, flexibility and adaptability, and a willingness to teach and be taught.

Table 4. Travel health insurance

Assistance:
    translators
    physician referral
    prescriptions
    medical monitoring
    medical evacuation
Health payments:
    direct
    reimbursement
    accidental death/amputation
Other:
    trip interruption
    baggage loss or damage

Table 5. Cultural adaptation (adapted from Ref. 40)

Country	Culture	Community	Work
Language	Attitudes	Housing	Skills
Politics	Values	Transport	Responsibilities
Geography	Dress	Communications	Schedule
Climate	Status of women	Schooling	Colleagues
Currency	Alcohol	Banking	No job
Instability/unrest		Shopping	
		Food	
		Friends	
		Sanitation	

After selection of the individual for an overseas assignment there are important aspects to preparing for this. Preparation should cover language skills, the foreign culture and local customs, geography and climate, and a realistic appraisal of the living and working environment.[41,42] Individuals should be advised to have 'tempered expectations', limit the number of initial tasks which they hope to accomplish, and to pursue a healthy lifestyle, with moderate consumption of alcohol. If the traveller has a spouse and/or children, they should be included in the training and planning process. It is important that they are involved in the choice of schooling and allowed to develop activities of interest. Leisure time with family should be built into any schedule. The possibility and pursuit of fulfilling work with new colleagues in a stimulating and challenging environment are important ingredients to successful residence in a new culture.

Health during travel

Infectious disease

This text devoted to travel medicine has clearly highlighted infectious health risks during travel — from the common disorder such as travellers' diarrhoea (Chapter 3) to the uncommon such as schistosomiasis, leishmaniasis and onchocerciasis (Chapter 8). By residing in the developing world for a prolonged period of time expatriate and long-term travellers have more frequent opportunities for exposure and are therefore at increased risk for both common and uncommon diseases compared with short-term travellers. Experience from the US Peace Corps (USPC) indicates that, in addition to diarrhoea, several problems are encountered more frequently in this group of young adults who usually reside in the developing world for two years (Fig. 1).[34,43,44]

Other less common infections may also be seen with higher frequency. As an example, HAV (Chapter 13), with a frequency of about one per 1,000 short-term travellers, is almost universal in missionaries serving for more than 20 years and occurs in about 25% of all missionaries.[45,46] HBV afflicts about 25% of missionaries and up to 50% of male expatriate workers in south-east Asia.[46,47] The availability of excellent protection against these infections should virtually eliminate both as a current risk. Cutaneous leishmaniasis (Chapter 8) is another uncommon infection which, while occurring in short-term travellers, is more frequently seen in those with repeated exposure over several months.[48,49]

The long-term traveller may also bring to light diseases which had not been previously recognised in an area. This has been well described with schistosomiasis in Lake Malawi, and *Plasmodium vivax* malaria in Somalia.[50,51] Expatriates had often considered Lake Malawi to be schistosomiasis-free, but a serostudy on 427 USPC and

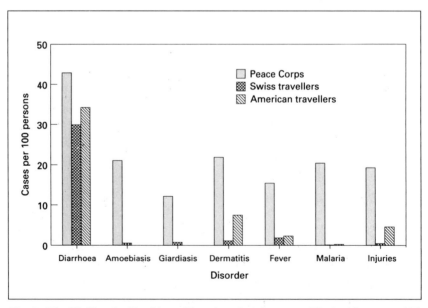

Fig 1. *The likelihood of health problems in selected groups. The incidence per 100 persons is indicated for three groups: United States Peace Corps volunteers,[44] Swiss travellers,[43] and American travellers.[34] For all conditions except diarrhoea, those with the longest period of exposure (the Peace Corps volunteers), have the highest incidence of the condition. (Incidence for Peace Corps volunteers is per year, and for Swiss and American travellers, per month and per three-week trip, respectively.)*

State Department personnel who swam in the lake demonstrated antibodies to *Schistosoma* spp in 33%.[50] In Somalia, the malaria prophylactic regimen employed was mefloquine or doxycycline, which targeted *P. falciparum* — the cause of nearly 95% of malaria infections in the region. However, following return to the USA, 77% (41/53) of malaria cases were caused by *P. vivax* due largely to the failure to include terminal chemotherapy with primaquine.[51]

Unusual manifestations of previously recognised or unrecognised pathogens can also occur. Five reported cases of a rare central nervous system complication of *Schistosoma* spp infection in those with water exposure, primarily in Lake Malawi, was particularly high and alerted health officials to the risk of schistosomiasis.[50,52,53] Unusual manifestations also occur when large numbers of individuals are exposed in a limited geographical area. Such a situation occurred when over 500,000 multinational troops were deployed in the Arabian peninsula during the Gulf War. In this instance, *Leishmania tropica,* which normally causes benign cutaneous disease, caused visceral leishmaniasis in several soldiers.[54] The possibility of unusual presentations is important for physicians who evaluate travellers both during their stay overseas and following return; they should be aware of the potential for these syndromes, and pursue appropriate diagnostic procedures.

Non-infectious illness

Although most travellers and physicians are concerned about infectious diseases during overseas travel, in reality these are the least common causes of serious morbidity and mortality, particularly for long-term and expatriate travellers. This is aptly illustrated in Chapter 6 on accidents and injuries, and by data on the reasons for repatriation (Table 6)[36,55] and overseas fatalities (Table 7).[56–59] The data for American and Scottish travellers, USPC volunteers and missionaries indicate that cardiovascular disease, vehicle accidents and sports injuries, malignancy, murder and suicide far exceed infectious diseases as causes of serious morbidity and mortality. Age-specific rates of illness differ, as reflected in the differences between American travellers and USPC volunteers — a younger group. Deaths from cardiovascular disease are highest in those over the age of 50, whereas deaths from accidents and injuries are highest in those under the age of 50.[57] Although little time is devoted during pre-travel preparations to general medical care and the avoidance of injury, it is imperative that organisations sending employees

Table 6. Reasons for repatriation

	Germans* (%)	Swedes** (%)
Accidental injuries	31	14
Medical diseases	28†	
Surgical disease		25
Infections	15	8
Lumbar disc problems	8	
Psychological disorders	8	16
Malignancy	5	
Gynaecological disorders	4	25
Miscellaneous		12††

* From Ref. 55: total number of workers was 1,550; 74 (4.9%) were repatriated during 1987–1990.
** From Ref. 36: total number of workers was 2,254; 51 (2.3%) were repatriated during 1974–1981.
† Includes both medical and surgical diseases.
†† Includes some medical diseases.

Table 7. Mortality overseas

Cause of death	Americans* (%)	Scots** (%)	Peace Corps† (%)	Missionaries††
Cardiovascular	49	69	6	3
Injury	22	21	69	1
Medical, other	14	6	3	4
Cancer	6	n.s.	1	2
Murder	2	n.s.	4	5
Suicide	1	n.s.	5	7
Infectious disease	1	4	5	6
Other/Unknown	6	1	7	

* From Ref. 56: 2,463 deaths were analysed for the years 1975 and 1984.
** From Ref. 57: 952 deaths were analysed for the years 1973–1988.
n.s., not stated.
† From Ref. 58: 185 deaths were analysed for the years 1962–1983.
†† From Ref. 59: missionary deaths for the years 1970–1985.
Deaths are in rank order, not per cent.

overseas are capable of screening for chronic disabling illness and of providing advice about personal safety. Personal safety would be much improved by combining safety information with recommendations about alcohol restraint, because many unintentional injuries are associated with alcohol consumption.

The returned traveller

Evaluation following return is the third important aspect of providing health care to travellers. Should all travellers or only selected individuals undergo screening following return? Strict criteria cannot be developed, but three groups may benefit from post-travel health care. The first group is the subject of this chapter — the long-term traveller and expatriate who has resided in the developing world for six or more months. These individuals have a higher cumulative risk of exposure to infectious agents, and in particular are likely to harbour intestinal helminths and protozoa.[36,60] A second group is those who had an illness during their trip, which was more serious than a mild case of travellers' diarrhoea or upper respiratory tract infection. Thirdly, any traveller who exhibits symptoms within several weeks — occasionally months or years — after return.

A careful history should be taken from each returned traveller, a physical examination performed, and selected laboratory tests requested.[61] Important features are the traveller's pre-travel preparations, including immunisation history and malaria prophylaxis, exposure risk and, finally, a clear description of the illness. For exposure risk, patients should be asked not only about their itinerary, but whether they undertook rural travel with potential exposure to leishmaniasis, schistosomiasis or filariasis. A sexual history should also be obtained. Based on this information, a predominant complaint or symptom such as abdominal pain, diarrhoea, fever, lymphadenopathy, skin rash or respiratory tract illness can usually be targeted. This will help to narrow the differential diagnoses and target laboratory investigations. Enquiry should always be made about illness in fellow travellers since some diseases may occur in clusters.

The physical examination will range from a screening examination for the asymptomatic returned traveller to an in-depth one focussing on the chief complaints in the sick traveller. A minimal examination consists of:

- vital signs;
- examination of the skin for rashes or insect bites;
- examination of the lymphatics for non-pitting oedema;
- auscultation of the heart and lungs;
- palpation of the abdomen to elicit abdominal discomfort; and
- assessment of the size of the liver and spleen.

A more detailed examination will be directed by the specific clinical features.

The first level of laboratory testing is based on the most likely diagnoses. This might include:

- full blood count;
- faecal examination of stools for ova, cysts and parasites;
- urinalysis;
- serum electrolytes; and
- liver function tests.

If the traveller is at risk, appropriate helminth serology should be obtained. All febrile patients should have a thick and thin blood smear examined because of the importance of malaria in returning travellers.[62-64] Further laboratory testing can usually be delayed until preliminary information has been obtained. All patients who have had either prolonged residence in the developing world, or possible exposure to people with tuberculosis should be screened for tuberculosis. If they have not received BCG vaccination, investigation can be carried out with purified protein derivative (PPD) skin testing approximately two months after return.[65]

A clinical diagnosis can usually be made once a careful history has been taken, physical examination performed and laboratory tests obtained. The predominant complaint may be a systemic illness involving a fever or exanthem, an organ-specific illness such as diarrhoea, jaundice or hepatosplenomegaly, or an isolated laboratory finding such as anaemia or eosinophilia. Each potential diagnosis should then be matched against its incubation period, its geographical area of risk, the frequency of occurrence in travellers and the pre-travel prevention measures, including compliance with anti-malarials (see above).[61] The incubation period can be particularly helpful when considering illness in the returned traveller (Table 8).[61,66] Many diseases can be readily excluded if their incubation period has been exceeded, while others may appear weeks to months and even years after exposure if their incubation is long — emphasising the necessity of a careful travel history in all patients.

The geographical distribution of illness is often difficult to assess accurately, but there are some guides to assist this.[13,66,67] It is important not to rule out a diagnosis based on geography alone since some diseases have occurred in areas previously considered free of infection. Diseases which are both common and widely distributed such as malaria, enteric infections and arboviral infections account for the majority of illness in returned travellers. However, when large numbers of individuals are concentrated in a small geographical area,

Table 8. Syndromes depending on incubation periods (adapted from Ref. 61)

Short (<7–10 days)	Intermediate	Long (>1 month)
Bacterial diarrhoea	Malaria	Malaria
Bacterial pneumonia	Enteric fever	Tuberculosis
Arbovirus infection	Giardiasis	Viral hepatitis
Rickettsial infection	Amoebiasis	Schistosomiasis
STDs* – gc, HSV, chlamydia, chancroid	Leptospirosis	Visceral leishmaniasis
Ebola/Marburg viruses	Lyme disease	Filariasis
Plague	Strongyloides	Helminths
	Lassa fever virus	Trypanosomiasis
	Trypanosomiasis	(*T.b. gambiense*)
	(*T.b. rhodesiense*)	Tropical sprue
	STDs – syphilis	Symptomatic HIV**
		Rabies

*STDs = Sexually transmitted diseases: gc = gonorrhoea; HSV = Herpes simplex virus. **HIV = Human immunodeficiency virus

even unusual infections can occur, as previously illustrated by the cluster of cases of visceral leishmaniasis in military personnel.[54]

The value of laboratory screening in healthy returned long-term and expatriate travellers is controversial. One study evaluated 1,029 individuals who had worked overseas for various UK organisations for three months to 45 years.[60] Full blood count, faecal microscopy for ova, cysts and parasites, and urinalysis (by dipstick) were performed on all travellers. Schistosomal and filarial serology was performed only on those at risk. Abnormalities were detected in nearly one-quarter of patients, but intervention was required in very few. Abnormal urinalysis was found in 24%, but none resulted from the tropical exposure. Faecal microscopy was abnormal in 19%, most of which, however, consisted of asymptomatic amoebiasis, giardiasis or blastocystosis (82%). There were a few cases of ascariasis, hookworm, strongyloidiasis and *Schistosoma* spp infection. Eosinophilia was detected in 16%, but only 3% overall had an eosinophilia secondary to one or more helminths, more than 65% being related to asymptomatic schistosomiasis. In only three of the cases in which a physical examination was carried out were findings revealed which had not been obtained either in the history or by laboratory testing. Similar findings on screening using faecal microscopy were recorded in Swedish workers in the tropics.[36]

Another study which evaluated the value of serology, faecal examination and eosinophil count in asymptomatic long-term returnees demonstrated that 75% of cases of eosinophilia were not associated with a parasitic disease.[68] Additionally, an eosinophil count as a single test was insensitive in identifying patients with strongyloidiasis, filariasis and schistosomiasis — confirming results of a previous study.[69] Combining an eosinophil count with faecal examination or serology, or performing serology and faecal tests together, proved more sensitive.[68]

These studies highlight two important points:

1. Many findings in asymptomatic returned travellers are not related to residence in the tropics. Perhaps it is more important to provide routine health care according to age-appropriate guidelines.
2. In only 5–15% of asymptomatic returned travellers are there abnormal findings related to overseas living which merit follow up and treatment.

Because of this relatively low yield, the cost-effectiveness of performing these screening tests will need to be decided by the responsible organisations and by the travellers themselves. Some organisations may decide to give their employees a 'clean bill of health' and perform the screening tests. Some travellers harbouring intestinal parasites will prefer to have themselves treated if they are not planning to return to the developing world. The use of post-travel or post-employment HIV testing should also be discussed.

Finally, many expatriates need to readjust to living in a 'western' society. This transition may be difficult, and for some will require both time and counselling. Others may have had disturbing experiences overseas — such as assault or serious illness. For each returned traveller, the experiences — both good and bad — will need to be discussed and dealt with.

Residence overseas for prolonged periods can bring many rewards in terms of cultural experience and job satisfaction, but it also presents challenges — both in preparing for life overseas and for maintaining health. Travel medicine physicians should be familiar with these issues in order to provide optimal care for long-term and expatriate travellers.

Acknowledgements

The author thanks Drs T Lankaster, C Dow and R Behrens for helpful discussions.

References

1. Hill DR. Pre-travel health, immunization status and demographics of travel of individuals visiting a travel medicine service. *American Journal of Tropical Medicine and Hygiene* 1991; **45**: 263–70
2. Barry M. Medical considerations for international travel with infants and older children. *Infectious Disease Clinics of North America* 1992; **6**: 389–404
3. Gillies P, Slack R, Stoddart N, Conway S. HIV-related risk behaviour in UK holiday-makers. *AIDS* 1992; **6**: 339–41
4. DeBuono BA, Zinner SH, Daamen M, McCormack WM. Sexual behavior of college women in 1975, 1986 and 1989. *New England Journal of Medicine* 1990; **322**: 821–5
5. Reid D, Cossar JH. Epidemiology of travel. *British Medical Bulletin* 1993; **49**: 257–68
6. Eyckmans L, Hill DR. Developing regions. In: DuPont HL, Steffen R (eds). *Travel medicine.* Decker Periodicals, (in press) 1995
7. Wilson ME, von Reyn CF, Fineberg HV. Infections in HIV-infected travelers: risks and prevention. *Annals of Internal Medicine* 1991; **114**: 582–92
8. von Reyn CF, Mann JM, Chin J. International travel and HIV infection. *Bulletin of the World Health Organization* 1990; **68**: 251–9
9. Hill DR. Immunizations. *Infectious Disease Clinics of North America* 1992; **6**: 291–312
10. Hill DR, Pearson RD. Measles prophylaxis for international travel (editorial). *Annals of Internal Medicine* 1989; **111**: 669–701
11. Centers for Disease Control and Prevention. Diphtheria outbreak — Russian Federation, 1990–1993. *Morbidity Mortality Weekly Report* 1993; **42**: 840–1
12. Parry JV, Perry KR, Mortimer PP, Farrington CP, *et al.* Rational programme for screening travellers for antibodies to hepatitis A virus. *Lancet* 1988; **i**: 1447–9
13. World Health Organization. *International travel and health. Vaccination requirements and health advice.* WHO: Geneva, 1994
14. Alonso PL, Lindsay SW, Armstrong Schellenberg JRM, Keita K, *et al.* A malaria control trial using insecticide-treated bed nets and targeted chemoprophylaxis in a rural area of The Gambia, West Africa. 6. The impact of the interventions on mortality and morbidity from malaria. *Transactions of the Royal Society of Tropical Medicine and Hygiene* 1993; **87** (Suppl 2): S37–44
15. Roland EH, Jan JE, Rigg JM. Toxic encephalopathy in a child after brief exposure to insect repellents. *Canadian Medical Association Journal* 1985; **132**: 155–6
16. Bradley D. Malaria Reference Laboratory and The Ross Institute. Prophylaxis against malaria for travellers from the United Kingdom. *British Medical Journal* 1993; **306**: 1247–52
17. Centers for Disease Control and Prevention. *Health information for international travel, 1994.* (HHS publication no. [CDC] 94–8280). Atlanta, GA: US Department of Health and Human Services, Public Health Service, 1994
18. Luzzi GA, Peto TEA. Adverse effects of anti-malarials. An update. *Drug Safety* 1993; **8**: 295–311

19. Easterbrook M. Dose relationships in patients with early chloroquine retinopathy. *Journal of Rheumatology* 1987; **14**: 472–5

20. Easterbrook M. Ocular effects and safety of antimalarial agents. *American Journal of Medicine* 1988; **85** (Suppl 4A): 23–9

21. Harries AD, Foreshaw CJ, Friend HM. Malaria prophylaxis amongst British residents of Lilongwe and Kasungu districts, Malawi. *Transactions of the Royal Society of Tropical Medicine and Hygiene* 1988; **82**: 690–2

22. Drysdale SF, Phillips-Howard PA, Behrens RH. Proguanil, chloroquine, and mouth ulcers. *Lancet* 1990; **i**: 164

23. Lobel HO, Miani M, Eng T, Bernard KW, *et al*. Long-term malaria prophylaxis with weekly mefloquine. *Lancet* 1993; **341**: 848–51

24. Steffen R, Fuchs E, Schildknecht J, Naef U, *et al*. Mefloquine compared with other malaria chemoprophylactic regimens in tourists visiting East Africa. *Lancet* 1993; **341**: 1299–303

25. White NJ. Mefloquine (editorial). *British Medical Journal* 1993; **308**: 286–7

26. Bem JL, Kerr L, Stuerchler D. Mefloquine prophylaxis: an overview of spontaneous reports of severe psychiatric reactions and convulsions. *Journal of Tropical Medicine and Hygiene* 1992; **95**: 167–79

27. Weinke T, Trautmann M, Held T, Weber G, *et al*. Neuropsychiatric side effects after the use of mefloquine. *American Journal of Tropical Medicine and Hygiene* 1991; **45**: 86–91

28. Pennie RA, Koren G, Crevoisier C. Steady state pharmacokinetics of mefloquine in long-term travellers. *Transactions of the Royal Society of Tropical Medicine and Hygiene* 1993; **87**: 459–62

29. Lobel HO, Campbell CC, Pappaioanou M, Huong AY. Use of prophylaxis for malaria by American travelers to Africa and Haiti. *Journal of the American Medical Association* 1987; **257**: 2626–7

30. Lobel HO, Phillips-Howard PA, Brandling-Bennett AD, Steffen R, *et al*. Malaria incidence and prevention among European and North American travellers to Kenya. *Bulletin of the World Health Organization* 1990; **68**: 209–15

31. Phillips-Howard PA, Blaze M, Hurn M, Bradley DJ. Malaria prophylaxis: survey of the response of British travellers to prophylactic advice. *British Medical Journal* 1986; **293**: 932–4

32. Steffen R, Heusser R, Mächler R, Bruppacher R, *et al*. Malaria chemoprophylaxis among European tourists in tropical Africa: use, adverse reactions, and efficacy. *Bulletin of the World Health Organization* 1990; **68**: 313–22

33. Fegan D, Glennon J. Malaria prophylaxis in long-term expatriate mineworkers in Ghana. *Occupational Medicine* 1993; **43**: 135–8

34. Hill DR. Illness associated with travel to the developing world. In: *Second Conference on International Travel Medicine*. Atlanta, GA: International Society of Travel Medicine, 1991: 71–3

35. DuPont HL, Ericsson CD. Prevention and treatment of traveler's diarrhea. *New England Journal of Medicine* 1993; **328**: 1821–7

36. Stenbeck JL. Health hazards in Swedish field personnel in the tropics *Travel Medicine International* 1991; **9**; 51–9

37. Beckham R. Holiday insurance. In: *Which?* 1990; February: 70–4

38. Fairhurst R. Health insurance for international travel. In: Dawood R

(ed). *Travellers' health. How to stay healthy abroad.* 3rd ed. Oxford: Oxford University Press, 1992; 371–5

39. Rose SR. *1994 International travel health guide.* Northampton, MA: Travel Medicine Inc, 1993
40. Sorti C. Culture shock and cultural adjustment: the psychological dimensions of the overseas sojourn. In: *Second Conference on International Travel Medicine.* Atlanta, GA: International Society of Travel Medicine, 1991: 20–1
41. Lankester T. *Healthy beyond Heathrow,* 2nd edn. London: InterHealth, 1994
42. Snashall D. Becoming an expatriate. In: Dawood R (ed). *Travellers' health. How to stay healthy abroad.* 3rd ed. Oxford: Oxford University Press, 1992: 363–70
43. Steffen R, Rickenbach M, Willhelm U, Helminger A, Schär M. Health problems after travel to developing countries. *Journal of Infectious Diseases* 1987; **156**: 84–91
44. Eng TR, Bernard KW, Banks D, van der Vlugt TB, Peace Corps Medical Officers. Epidemiologic surveillance of health conditions among temporary residents of developing countries: the Peace Corps experience. In: *Second Conference on International Travel Medicine* Atlanta, GA: International Society of Travel Medicine, 1991: 16–9
45. Steffen R. Risk of hepatitis A in travellers. *Vaccine* 1992; **10** (Suppl 1): S69–72
46. Lange WR, Frame JD. High incidence of viral hepatitis among American missionaries in Africa. *American Journal of Tropical Medicine and Hygiene* 1990; **43**: 527–33
47. Dawson DG, Spivey GH, Korelitz JJ, Schmidt RT. Hepatitis B: risk to expatriates in South East Asia. *British Medical Journal* 1987; **294**: 547
48. Herwaldt BL, Stokes SL, Juranek DD. American cutaneous leishmaniasis in US travelers. *Annals of Internal Medicine* 1993; **118**: 779–84
49. Melby PC, Kreutzer RD, McMahon-Pratt D, Gam AA, Neva FA. Cutaneous leishmaniasis: review of 59 cases seen at the National Institutes of Health. *Journal of Infectious Diseases* 1992; **15**: 924–37
50. Centers for Disease Control and Prevention. Schistosomiasis in US Peace Corps volunteers — Malawi, 1992. *Morbidity Mortality Weekly Report* 1993; **42**: 565–70
51. Centers for Disease Control and Prevention. Malaria among US military personnel returning from Somalia, 1993. *Morbidity Mortality Weekly Report* 1993; **42**: 524–6
52. Blanchard TJ, Milne LM, Pollok R, Cook GC. Early chemotherapy of imported neuroschistosomiasis (letter). *Lancet* 1993; **341**: 959
53. Blunt SB, Boulton J, Wise R. MRI in schistosomiasis of conus medullaris and lumbar spinal cord. *Lancet* 1993; **341**: 557
54. Magill AJ, Grögl M, Gasser RA, Wellington S, Oster CN. Visceral infection caused by *Leishmania tropica* in veterans of Operation Desert Storm. *New England Journal of Medicine* 1993; **328**: 1383–7
55. Mikulicz U. Screening for physical and psychological fitness of persons going to the tropics for a prolonged period. In: *Second Conference on International Travel Medicine.* Atlanta, GA: International Society of Travel Medicine, 1991; 22–4

56. Hargarten SW, Baker T, Guptill K. Fatalities of American travelers —
    1975 and 1984. In: *First Conference on International Travel Medicine*.
    Zürich, Switzerland: Springer-Verlag, 1988; 55–60
57. Paixao MLTD, Dewar RD, Cossar JH, Covell RG, Reid D. What do
    Scots die of when abroad? *Scottish Medical Journal* 1991; **36**: 114–6
58. Hargarten SW, Baker SP. Fatalities in the Peace Corps: a retrospective
    study: 1962 through 1983. *Journal of the American Medical Association*
    1985; **254**: 1326–9
59. Frame JD, Lange WR, Frankenfield DL. Mortality trends of American
    missionaries in Africa, 1945–1985. *American Journal of Tropical Medicine
    and Hygiene* 1992; **46**: 686–90
60. Carroll B, Dow C, Snashall D, Marshall T, Chiodini PL. Post-tropical
    screening: how useful is it? *British Medical Journal* 1993; **307**: 541
61. Hill DR. Evaluation of the returned traveler. *Yale Journal of Biology and
    Medicine* 1992; **65**: 343–56
62. Phillips-Howard PA, Radalowicz J, Mitchell J, Bradley DJ. Risk of
    malaria in British residents returning from malarious areas. *British
    Medical Journal* 1990; **300**: 499–503
63. Greenberg AE, Lobel HO. Mortality from *Plasmodium falciparum*
    malaria in travelers from the United States, 1959 to 1987. *Annals of
    Internal Medicine* 1990; **113**: 326–7
64. Bradley DJ, Warhurst DC. Malaria imported into the United Kingdom
    during 1991. *Communicable Disease Report* 1993; **3**: (Rev no. 2): R25–8
65. Immunization Practices Advisory Committee (ACIP). Use of BCG
    vaccines in the control of tuberculosis: A joint statement of the ACIP
    and the advisory committee for elimination of tuberculosis. *Morbidity
    Mortality Weekly Report* 1988; **37**: 663–4, 669–75
66. Wilson ME. *A world guide to infections. Diseases, distribution, diagnosis*.
    Oxford: Oxford University Press, 1991
67. Beal CB, Lyerly WH. Global epidemiology of infectious disease. In:
    Strickland GT (ed). *Hunter's Tropical Medicine*. 7th ed. Philadelphia:
    WB Saunders Company, 1991: 1048–74
68. Libman MD, MacLean JD, Gyorkos TW. Screening for schistosomia-
    sis, filariasis, and strongyloidiasis among expatriates from the tropics.
    Clinical Infectious Diseases 1993; **17**: 353–9
69. Fryatt RJ, Teng J, Harries AD, Siorvanes L, Hall AP. Intestinal
    helminthiasis in expatriates returning to Britain from the tropics. A
    controlled study. *Tropical and Geographical Medicine* 1990; **42**: 119–22

11 | Prevention of disease in travellers

Robert Steffen
Head of Division of Communicable Diseases, Institute of Social and Preventive Medicine, Zurich University, Switzerland

The raison d'être of travel medicine is to keep travellers healthy. To achieve this goal, we must be aware of the health risks, reviewed in Chapters 1–3 and elsewhere.[1] This awareness should not be limited to disease prevention. Accidents are also important (Chapter 6); for example, it has been shown that traffic and swimming accidents are the main cause of death in foreigners in Mexico.[2,3]

Two basic rules must be observed in preventive travel medicine: *primum non nocere* (first, do no harm) is paramount, even more so than in curative medicine where risks sometimes have to be taken.[4] With all prophylactic measures the benefit of avoidance of disease — usually an infection, must clearly exceed the risk of adverse events on a community health scale. Above all, chemoprophylaxis and/or vaccines should not be prescribed when there will be no risk of exposure; in this situation, the benefit is zero and the cost may occasionally be a fatal adverse reaction.[5]

The optimum level of protection may be debated. Essentially, it is a question of how much a traveller is willing to pay. Priorities are important, and prevention should never be recommended against rare risks while leaving the prospective traveller unprotected against more frequently occurring diseases of comparable severity.

To recommend targeted preventive measures, basic information is required on:

- *the traveller:* age, sex, weight, relevant host factors such as pregnancy, recent and chronic diseases — particularly allergies and those requiring medication (special risk groups will not be addressed in this review);
- *travel plans:* destination, duration, travel style;
- *the environment:* epidemiological situation at the destination, including resistance to drugs, seasonality and basic cultural aspects.

Important preventive measures will be discussed not by disease, but by the type(s) of measures undertaken.

Information for the traveller

Travellers require a certain amount of knowledge concerning travel health. Unless they understand a danger, they will not try to reduce the risks. Many physicians and nurses lack the time and patience to teach each traveller individually (large travel clinics advise up to 50,000 travellers annually) but such knowledge can be transmitted by videos, brochures, books[6] or other media. The counselling medical professional should, however, set priorities and ensure that these important messages have been understood; these include awareness about the risk, and knowledge about measures to be taken.

Minimising exposure to risks of travel

Travel (French, *travail*) means work. Various forms of environmental stress may impair well-being and reduce 'resistance' to disease. Major risks can be avoided to a large extent (Table 1). Two of these avoidance measures will be described in detail.

In most travellers, protective measures against arthropod transmission of a wide variety of communicable diseases will concentrate on the period between dusk and dawn — largely to avoid malaria (Chapter 2).[10] Although living entirely in air conditioned or screened rooms may be 'safe', few tourists will completely renounce outdoor activities. Thus, advice on exposure prevention is important: the arms, legs and particularly the ankles should be covered. Mosquito bites penetrate light-weight fabrics (< 1 mm thick and opening > 0.1 mm[11]). Clothing can be sprayed with permethrin insecticides which, when used as directed, provide residual protection for up to two weeks. While dark colours attract *Anopheles* spp, light ones attract *Aedes* spp mosquitoes.[11] An insect repellent containing N, N diethyl-m-toluamide (DEET) should be applied to exposed skin; the concentration is limited to 35% in many countries due to possible toxicity — a concern especially in infants.[12] Older DEET formulations are rapidly lost through perspiration, but new ones containing polymers (eg 'Ultrathon 3M') persist, although frequently perceived as sticky. Even in air conditioned rooms, the occasional mosquito may enter, and it is advisable to use an insecticide spray before retiring for the night. When accommodation allows entry of mosquitoes, sprays, dispensers or pyrethroid mosquito coils should be used — in addition to a mosquito net. Impregnation with permethrin will further increase the protective effect.[13,14]

Table 1. Reducing exposure to risks

Risk category	Type	Effective prevention
Environment	Stress	allow sufficient time
– air/sea travel	Claustro-, agarophobia	seat selection; programme of brief cognitive therapy[7]
	Motion sickness	avoid small boats and planes, seat selection, etc
	Circadian dysrhythmia	rest, short-acting sleeping pill?[8] (future: melatonin?)
– at destination	Climate: heat/cold, humidity, dehydration	adequate clothing; push fluids and mineral salts; regular showers; avoid excessive exertion
	Sun	filter sun cream; initially minimal exposure
	Freshwater	do not expose — to avoid schistosomiasis; pools safe (?)
	Saltwater	avoid currents, rather swim than wade; wear shoes
	Soil	to avoid parasites neither walk barefoot nor lie on the soil
	Culture	psychological screening for long-term residents
	Altitude	slow ascent if possible; warn high-risk subjects
	Traffic	avoid travelling at night; avoid motor bicycles; wear seat-belts
Human–human	Sexually transmitted diseases	avoid unprotected casual sex
Animal–human	Rabies	neither pet unknown animals, nor touch cadavers
	Snakes (rare), scorpions	wear closed shoes; inspect clothing before dressing
	Jellyfish, poisonous fish	ask natives; wear goggles if necessary
Vector-borne	Malaria, dengue, etc.	measures against mosquito bites
Food-borne	Travellers' diarrhoea, etc.	'boil it, cook it, peel it, or forget it' — as far as possible
Intoxicant drugs	Alcohol, marijuana, etc.	avoid having impaired judgement before sex, swimming, diving, etc[9]

Almost all experts advising travellers recommend the avoidance of contaminated food (Chapter 3), but virtually no one adheres faithfully to such advice, although clear-cut evidence for its efficacy has been demonstrated.[15] Very few travellers (except the eminent

diarrhoea researcher Herbert DuPont) test the food served with a
thermometer and refuse it unless the core temperature is at least
60°C. Such careful behaviour will reduce the size of the inoculum
of infectious organisms ingested but, for the most part, the advice
is not practical and will not completely protect individuals from
gastrointestinal infections;[16] pathogens are sometimes found even
in recommended food and beverages — such as melon into which
water has been injected to increase the weight[17], or bottled water.[18]

Human fallibility is also important; it will not be possible either
to convince travellers to abstain completely from cold buffet
luncheons or other potentially contaminated food, or in the near
future to have a hygienically satisfactory situation in all kitchens in
developing countries.

A new strategy is necessary. Travellers should be taught about
the risk scale (Fig 1). Emphasis should be placed on encouraging
individuals to abstain from highly dangerous items and situations.
Every traveller is free to decide what risks he or she wishes to take,
but it should be an *informed* decision.

Chemoprophylaxis

Malaria (see also Chapters 2 and 10)

Malaria chemoprophylaxis is a 'suppressive' strategy; thus, medication must be started one week prior to departure (to check tolerance and, in the case of some drugs, to ensure that they reach a
therapeutic range[19]), and continued during the stay in the endemic country, and for four weeks thereafter. Experience shows

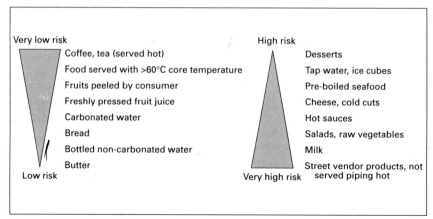

Fig 1. *Risk of contamination of food and beverages.*

that compliance is poor in this final, post-exposure phase, so it may be useful to explain the rationale in simple terms: that the parasites move from the liver into the red blood cells and can be attacked only at this time. According to the World Health Organization (WHO), options for chemoprophylaxis are limited to chloroquine (CQ), chloroquine plus proguanil (CQ+PG =CP), doxycycline (DX) and mefloquine (MQ). Effectiveness, which is never complete, and the incidence of adverse events — which is far from zero, are compared in Figure 2 and Table 2.

Two non-randomised studies shown in Figure 2 illustrate the superiority of MQ as compared to CP or CQ in sub-Saharan Africa.[20,21] It should be noted that neither CQ nor CP prophylaxis prevented a fatal outcome.[21,23] In addition, a randomised Dutch trial compared CP in two dosages and monoprophylaxis with PG 200 mg daily in travellers staying in sub-Saharan Africa (there was no mefloquine group for comparison).[24] Malaria was proven in only 12 patients and no significant differences were detected in this study. The authors' conclusion that the CP combination can still be recommended for visitors to east, central and southern

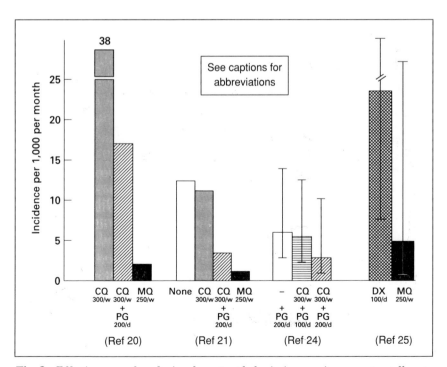

Fig 2. *Effectiveness of malaria chemoprophylaxis in non-immune travellers to tropical Africa.* CQ: chloroquine; DX; doxycycline; MQ; mefloquine; PG: proguanil; d: day; w: week.

Africa is unwarranted. Further studies compared DX, apparently as ineffective a causal prophylactic agent as any other, and MQ in US Armed Forces in Somalia.[25,26]

Transmission of malaria is lower in frequently visited parts of south-east Asia and South America and no recent comparative studies have been conducted in non-immune civilian populations. *In vitro* monitoring of sensitivity showed a marked increase of MQ resistance in Thailand around 1990,[27, 28] particularly along the Cambodian and Burmese borders. These alarming results were probably influenced by being based on patients in third-line medical institutions. In contrast, Dutch marines operating as part

Table 2. Adverse effects of agents recommended by the World Health Organization for chemoprophylaxis of malaria in non-immune individuals (see caption for abbreviations)

| Agent | No. | Total | Adverse events | | Reference |
			Most frequent	Serious	
CP, CQ	520	45.8	Strange dreams, nausea	none	20
MQ	802	40.6	Strange dreams, insomnia	none	
None	4,026	0			21
CQ	3,354	17.2	Nausea, headache, dizziness	seizures, psychosis*	
CP	20,150	30.1	Nausea, mouth ulcers, headache	psychosis*	
MQ	50,053	18.7	Nausea, dizziness, headache	seizures, psychosis*	
CQ	156	46 CNS	Insomnia, headache, dizziness	none	22
		31 GI	Nausea, diarrhoea, abdominal pain		
MQ	157	43 CNS	Insomnia, headache, dreams	none	
		27 GI	Nausea, diarrhoea, vomiting		

*	= 1 in 10,000 approximately
CP	= chloroquine + proguanil
CQ	= chloroquine
MQ	= mefloquine
CNS	= central nervous system
GI	= gastrointestinal

of the United Nations Transitional Authority for Cambodia (UNTAC) peace-keeping force were well protected by MQ, except immediately after deployment and prior to having attained adequate MQ blood levels.[29] It may well be that not only did improved efficacy of MQ play a decisive role, but also that compliance with a weekly regimen is usually significantly better than with either a daily one, or the complex CP regimen.[20,21,25]

The bad reputation which malaria chemoprophylaxis has for adverse events among the public is confirmed by questionnaire surveys and controlled studies (Table 2). The rate of mild to moderate side-effects is high with all regimens and results in discontinuation of chemoprophylaxis in 2–3%. CQ and MQ have similar rates of adverse events both in open and in double-blind studies, whereas that for CP was markedly higher than for MQ in the open trials.[20–22] Both CQ and MQ result in serious neuropsychiatric toxicity in approximately one per 10,000 prophylactic users.

Which agent should be chosen on the basis of these findings? As suggested by the WHO (Fig 3),[30] MQ is preferred for most areas with high transmission of chloroquine-resistant *Plasmodium falciparum*, while CQ continues to be the drug of choice where no resistance exists. In areas of intermediate risk, CP is the preferred regimen. In areas with low transmission, some experts prefer to recommend measures against mosquito bites only, and to refrain from chemoprophylaxis but provide the traveller with a 'stand-by' regimen for emergencies.

This Chapter is concerned with disease *prevention* and does not include self-treatment to minimise complications of disease abroad, but the pros and cons of such a strategy have been discussed elsewhere.[31]

Travellers' diarrhoea (see also Chapter 3)

Effective ways of preventing travellers' diarrhoea have been a priority for a long time and many drugs have been considered. Many antimicrobial agents have been demonstrated to be effective (for review, see Ref. 32); preference is now given to the fluoroquinolones which may be used for periods up to three weeks. In contrast, probiotics such as *Lactobacillus* spp[32,33] and *Saccharomyces boulardii*[34,35] were either not significantly or satisfactorily effective. Bismuth subsalicylate has an intermediate position, with a modest efficacy of 35–65%.[36,37]

Most travellers should not take antimicrobial chemoprophylaxis for prevention of travellers' diarrhoea because of potential

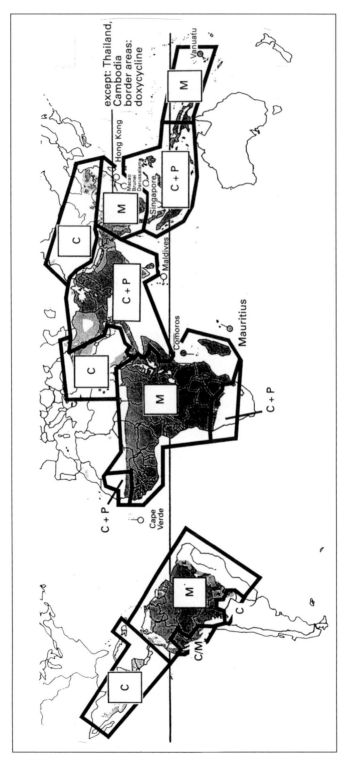

Fig 3. *Malaria chemoprophylactic regimens recommended by the World Health Organization (1994). C: chloroquine; C + P: chloroquine + proguanil; M: mefloquine.*

side-effects, cost, a false sense of security which is given by such medication, and the resultant uncertainty about how to treat diarrhoea which might still develop. Chemoprophylaxis of travellers' diarrhoea is frequently practised in the USA,[38] but almost all European experts limit its use to clearly defined groups. These include:

- individuals with an increased susceptibility to travellers' diarrhoea, such as a history of repeated severe illness during previous journeys;
- those with an impaired gastric acid barrier (caused by omeprazole, some antacids, gastrectomy, etc);
- individuals with an increased risk of complications — in whom dehydration or electrolyte imbalance could have serious consequences; and
- VIPs who have to accept whatever is offered, but nevertheless be able to 'perform' without interruption.

Motion sickness

A variety of drugs has comparable efficacy in motion sickness and a comparable rate of adverse events, notably tiredness — as recently demonstrated during a large trial conducted with whale safari tourists in Norway (Fig 4).[39] No significant differences were detected in this trial; therefore any of the available agents may be recommended, and the decision will usually be influenced by a previous favourable experience by the individual traveller. Scopolamine TTS tends to be slightly less efficient and results in a higher rate of adverse effects.[40]

High altitude illness

In individuals who plan a rapid ascent to altitudes above 1,000 m, especially when tolerance to hypoxia is diminished, acetazolamide chemoprophylaxis can be recommended.[41] Common side-effects include parasthesiae in the fingers and face. Since the agent is contra-indicated in those who are allergic to sulphur compounds dexamethasone is an alternative agent. Nifedipidine should be reserved for those who have previously experienced high altitude illness.[42]

Immunisation prophylaxis

When advising travellers, it is essential to differentiate between routine, mandatory and advised vaccinations. Wide variations in vaccination rates in travellers originating from different countries

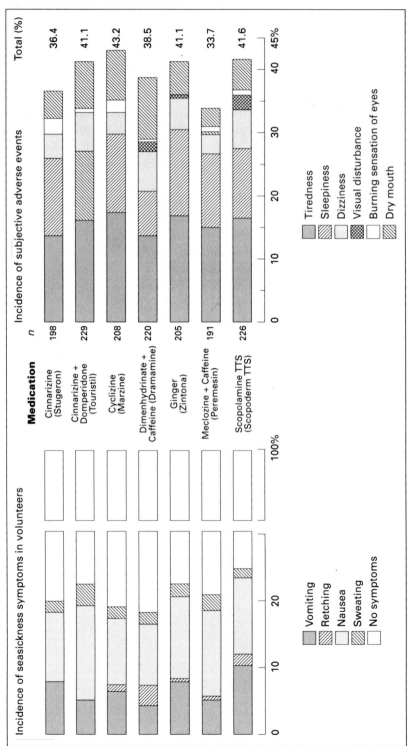

Fig 4. *Efficacy and tolerance of anti-motion sickness drugs.*

illustrate the need for a consensus of opinion.[43] Characteristics of various vaccines are summarised in Table 3.

Routine vaccinations

Tetanus, diphtheria, poliomyelitis and measles/mumps/rubella may all be a risk to travellers. Everyone should be protected, whether or not they travel.

Mandatory vaccinations

According to the International Health Regulations, only vaccination against yellow fever should be mandatory.[14] Authorities in various countries in tropical Africa and South America require proof of vaccination from all visitors. Additional countries —

Table 3. Synopsis of vaccines for use by travellers

Indication	Route	Regimen (days)	Efficacy (%)	Effective from day*	Duration of protection
Cholera					
(WC inactivated)	ID/SC/IM	0/(28 optional)	50	P6, R1	O:6m, E:3–4m
(CVD-103HgR)	PO (CVD-103HgR)	0	80	P6, R1	O/E: 6 m
Diphtheria	IM	0 (B)	80	15	5(–10) y
Yellow fever	SC	0	> 99	P10, R1	O: 10y, E: >15y
Hepatitis A					
(active)	IM	0/(14–30†)/180–365	98	< 14	10–25 y
(Ig, passive)	IM	0	85	2	3–5 m
Hepatitis B	IM	0/14–30/180–365	90	30	3–8 y
Japanese encephalitis	IM	0/7–14 (14–28)/365	90	7	1–4 y
Measles	SC	0	90	30	Usually >20 y
Meningococcal					
meningitis	IM	0	70–90	7	1–3 y
Poliomyelitis	PO	0 (B)	>99	30	10 y
	IM		>99	30	5(–10) y
Rabies	IM/ID	0/7/21–28	>99	7	2–3 y
Tetanus	IM	0 (B)	>99	15	10 y
Tuberculosis	ID	0	50	60	10 (?) y
Typhoid fever					
(Ty21a)	PO	0/2/4	70	15	1(–7) y
(TAB)	IM	0/28	70	15	2–7 y
(ViCPS)	IM	0	70	< 28	> 3 y

* if more than one dose necessary, number of days after completion of series.
Ig: immunoglobulin; ID: intradermal; SC: subcutaneous; IM: intramuscular; PO: by mouth; B: only booster needed; P: primary vaccination; R: revaccination; O: official; E: effective; m: months; y: years.
† Havrix® 720 EL units; unnecessary if 1,440 EL units used.

including some in Asia — also have this requirement, fearing that this arbovirus infection, which has a high fatality rate, might be imported by those who have arrived from an endemic area. The 'official' endemic areas and those with reported infections in the past 20 years are shown in Figure 5; however, the actual areas of virus activity far exceed these zones. Yellow fever epidemics can suddenly flare up without warning as occurred recently in Kenya which had not experienced such an event for 50 years.[44]

The yellow fever vaccine is one of the few live attenuated vaccines used in travel medicine; it is almost 100% effective.[45] Usually well tolerated, it may cause systemic reactions in 5–25% of recipients, but only 0.2% are to some extent incapacitated.[46] The vaccine is cultured in chick embryos, and is contra-indicated in individuals with an allergy to eggs, children less than six (12 in some countries) months of age — due to an increased risk of encephalitis — and those who are immunosuppressed as a result of either disease or therapy (including high corticosteroid doses). In pregnancy and asymptomatic HIV-positive individuals, the risk of infection should be weighed against the theoretical risk of vaccination. If a traveller is unable to take the vaccine despite the official requirement, a medical certificate should be issued, which is validated by an official vaccinating centre.

Vaccinations — advised against frequent risks

Hepatitis A (HAV). Several inactivated and attenuated HAV vaccines have been developed in recent years against this vaccine-preventable disease in travellers (Fig 6) (see also Chapter 13).[47,48] An inactivated vaccine based on strain HM 175 (Havrix®, SmithKline Beecham Biologicals) has been marketed in Europe since January 1992. (Characteristics, production and quality control of this vaccine have been described elsewhere.[49]) With a dose of 720 EL units, two doses (initially and at one month) followed by a booster dose at 6–12 months are recommended. A 1,440 EL unit dose has recently been introduced, single administration inducing a 77–100% seroconversion rate at day 14,[50,51] the lowest seroconversion being found in the 40–62 year age group.[52] A single dose gives a seroconversion rate of 100 and 95%, respectively, at months seven and 12, while a booster dose at 6–12 months will protect for an estimated 10–25 years[53,54] according to a mathematical model of vaccine-induced antibody decay.

Tolerance to this vaccine has been similar in type, frequency, severity and duration to that obtained with recombinant DNA

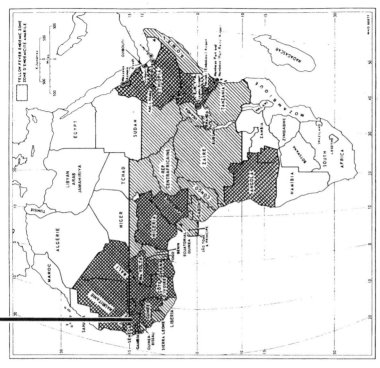

Fig 5. *Yellow fever infected and endemic areas (1973–1993).*

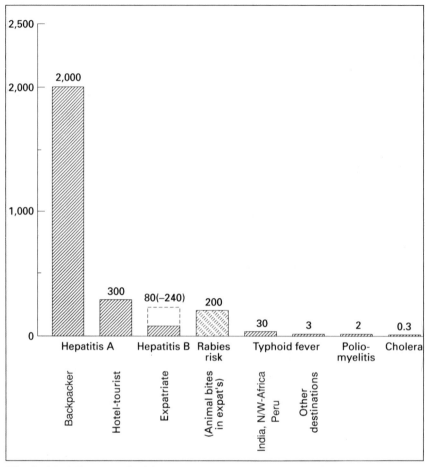

Fig 6. *Morbidity per 100,000 travellers of vaccine-preventable infections in non-immune travellers.*

yeast-derived hepatitis A (HAV) vaccine.[55] The claimed probable association of transient encephalopathy with HAV vaccination is unsubstantiated since it is uncertain to what extent other possible causes were adequately excluded.[56] The active vaccine offers a higher protection rate for a longer period than immunoglobulin, which does not apparently protect against fulminant fatal hepatitis A, as shown in a young British traveller.[57, 58] The anti-HAV content of some immunoglobulins prepared in industrialised countries has decreased below 100 IU/ml. For some unsubstantiated reason(s) many individuals are reluctant to receive a blood-derived product.

If departure is scheduled for ≤ 14 days after a first dose of HAV vaccine, active/passive immunisation may be considered. However, this is followed by a depressed immune response to HAV vaccine,[59,60] and protection by the initial vaccine dose may occur before seroconversion can be demonstrated. For residents of a country with low endemicity who visit a high-risk area, active vaccine is more cost-effective than immunoglobulin if three or more journeys in the next ten-year period, are planned, or if the total duration of stay abroad is to exceed 180 days. If testing is readily available, and there is enough time to wait for results, pre-screening for anti-HAV antibody may be cost-effective for individuals born before 1945 (later in some regions), those with a history of jaundice, and who have lived for more than one year in a developing country.[61, 62] Individuals without such a history may receive HAV vaccine without pre-screening, since it is well tolerated by seropositive individuals.

Hepatitis B (HBV). Various human plasma-derived inactivated viral vaccines, and increasingly, recombinant DNA vaccines, are marketed (Chapter 13); they have differing schedules. With rare exceptions, the vaccines are well tolerated and there are no specific contra-indications.[63] There is a higher proportion of slow or non-responders with increasing age and in people who consume excessive alcohol.[64] It may be worth assessing anti-HBs titres in these groups prior to departure in order to be able to recommend additional booster doses if/when necessary. In contrast to long-term residents, tourists are rarely affected by HBV unless they break basic hygienic rules, such as having acupuncture or tattoos, or indulge in unprotected casual sex, etc; some however, may be infected by medical or dental treatment.[65] Indications for vaccination in sex-tourists are questionable; it may give a dangerous sense of security and increase the risk of HIV infection.

Rabies. Vaccines used against this long underestimated risk commonly cause mild to moderate local reactions, but systemic reactions occur in only 0.2–5% — mainly urticaria, fever, arthralgias, nausea and, rarely, the Guillain Barré syndrome — developing up to three weeks after vaccination.[66, 67] There are no specific contra-indications. Pre-exposure prophylaxis does *not* eliminate the need for post-exposure treatment, but it is generally agreed that it simplifies the latter by eliminating the need for rabies immunoglobulin.[68,69] Intradermal vaccination is cheaper if a single vial can be used simultaneously for a group of travellers, but this may compromise vaccine efficacy — as may co-medication with chloroquine within three weeks of the third dose.[68,70]

Typhoid fever. Travellers at highest risk are those eating and drinking off the beaten track, those visiting high-risk countries (Fig 6), and those with a prolonged exposure to potentially contaminated food. Three vaccines are now available (Table 3). They all claim to have a similar efficacy against *Salmonella typhi* infection only, but this has never been verified in non-immune travellers.[71, 72] If oral Ty21a vaccine is used, particular emphasis should be placed on cool storage and ingestion on an empty stomach.[73] Antimalarial agents and antibiotics may inactivate Ty21a.[74] TAB vaccine was associated with pronounced local pain and occasionally serious adverse effects,[75, 76] while Ty21a vaccine may occasionally cause diarrhoea. Both vaccines are contra-indicated if adverse effects occurred previously; Ty21a vaccine is also contra-indicated in individuals with an acute intestinal infection, infants less than three months old, and pregnant and nursing women (mainly due to lack of experience).

Influenza. Except for anecdotal reports of epidemics which occurred after a prolonged stay in an aircraft,[17] there are no surveys comparing the risk in travellers with that in non-travellers. Older travellers in particular, may be at risk of complications.

Vaccinations — occasionally advised against rare risks

Meningococcal disease. This vaccination is required for the pilgrimage to Mecca, Saudi Arabia, because several oubreaks have occurred. At-risk travellers are impossible to determine in advance. The vaccine is indicated for travellers to areas with epidemic outbreaks, particularly if they live closely with the 'natives', and/or if they have been splenectomised.[78] Despite an epidemic, no infections have been reported in almost one million tourists visiting Kenya each year.[79] The presently marketed vaccine provides immunity against serogroups A, C, and partly Y and W-135, but not serogroup B (which is the dominant strain in Europe).

Japanese encephalitis. This mosquito-borne virus infection occurs in south, south-east and north-east Asia, mainly in summer and autumn.[80,81] Individuals at risk are particularly those who spend day and night for several weeks in rural endemic areas;[80] the risk for the average tourist or business traveller is extremely low. The vaccine is not licensed in most European countries but can be obtained in many travel clinics.[82] It has recently been associated with serious adverse reactions,[83] and is thus reserved for 'high risk' travellers (eg back-packers to rural areas of south-east Asia).

Cholera. This infection affects primarily the lower socio-economic strata of endemic countries; tourists are rarely affected.[84] All expert groups emphasise that hygienic measures are far more important than vaccination. According to the Travel Information Manual issued monthly by airlines,[85] only the islands of Zanzibar and Pemba, Tanzania, still require proof of vaccination; there are nowadays only rare reports about similar requirements at remote border posts. The traditional inactivated whole-cell vaccine provides an unsatisfactory efficacy of 50%; the newly introduced CVD-103HgR oral vaccine (Table 3) is more reliable.[86,87] However, neither is indicated in travellers.

Tick-borne encephalitis. This infection is a risk for individuals travelling cross-country through undergrowth in many parts of continental Europe, mainly Austria, Germany, German-speaking parts of Switzerland, Slovakia and Hungary. Only a minority (0.1–1%) of ticks are infected and meningo-encephalitis develops in only 1–10% of infected individuals.[88] Two vaccines are available, and these have occasionally been associated with adverse neurological effects.[89] If exposure is highly likely, the vaccine may be combined with specific immunoglobulin.

Tuberculosis. Prolonged close exposure is necessary for infection and, as only limited protection is offered,[90] this vaccine is indicated for travellers only exceptionally.

Pneumococcal disease. Pneumococcal vaccine is indicated for any patient with individual risk factors for invasive disease, but there is no evidence to support the view that travellers to Spain should be immunised routinely.[91]

Plague. The risk to travellers is virtually non-existent: no case of plague has been imported into the UK since 1918.[92] The epidemic which occurred in India in the autumn of 1994 did not affect a single traveller; it is questionable whether this epidemic was true plague, since WHO experts were unable to detect *Yersinia pestis* in any sample.

Recommendations and conclusions

The counselling medical professional should decide which immunisation(s) to recommend for a traveller. The travel agent, embassy official or staff at a national tourist office should not be involved; they tend to mention only the mandatory immunisations corresponding to the minimum requirement as decreed by law.[93]

Overall no vaccination in travellers is 'cost-saving',[94] but some may well be worth the additional cost for the individual. It is not usually necessary to immunise future travellers with all available vaccines; a practising physician concerned about being sued unless he or she gives the entire choice of vaccines is ill informed. WHO and various national expert groups have formulated concise and logical recommendations as to which traveller should get which vaccine — based on the above-mentioned epidemiological data (Table 4).

Ideally, all travellers should consult a travel clinic or competent physician 4–6 weeks prior to departure (the exception is yellow fever vaccine which is given at a specially licensed centre). All the vaccines can frequently be given at a single visit, but travellers requiring immunisation against HBV, rabies, Japanese encephalitis,

Table 4. Recommended immunisations prior to a stay in a developing country (World Health Organization[14])

Immunisation	Indication	
Poliomyelitis Tetanus, Diphtheria Measles Hepatitis A*	+	for all travellers
Yellow fever	+	when required
	+	recommended for all visits to endemic areas
Hepatitis B	(+)	'extended or frequent travel to countries of high endemicity'
Typhoid fever	(+)	'conditions of doubtful hygiene'
Rabies	(+)	'≥1 month . . . where rabies is . . . threat'
Meningococcal disease	(+)	'hyperendemic areas in close contact with local population'
Japanese encephalitis	(+)	'extended stay in rural areas of endemic countries'
Influenza	(+)	'elderly . . . and . . . high-risk medical condition'
BCG	(+)	'children and young adults . . . extended stay'
Cholera	–	'not recommended as means of personal protection'

* = Vaccine is preferred when available
+ = recommended
(+) = recommended for special situations
– = not recommended

and individuals who have not received a primary series of poliomyelitis, tetanus and diphtheria vaccines may require up to three visits. Interactions between vaccines have now become irrelevant unless immunoglobulin is still used.

References:

1. Steffen R, Lobel HO. Epidemiological basis for the practice of travel medicine. *Wilderness Medicine* 1994; **5**: 56–66
2. Guptill KS, Hargarten SW, Baker TD. American travel death in Mexico: causes and prevention strategies. *Western Journal of Medicine* 1991; **154**: 169–71
3. Hargarten SW, Baker TD, Guptill KS. Overseas fatalities of United States citizen travelers: an analysis of death related to international travel. *Annals of Emergency Medicine* 1991; **20**: 622–6
4. Sox HC. Preventive health services in adults. *New England Journal of Medicine* 1994; **330**: 1589–95
5. Miller KD, Lobel HO, Satriale RF, *et al.* Severe cutaneous reactions among American travelers using pyrimethamine-sulfadoxine (Fansidar®) for malaria prophylaxis. *American Journal of Tropical Medicine and Hygiene* 1986; **35**: 451–8
6. Dawood R (ed). *Travellers' health: how to stay healthy abroad*, 3rd edn. New York: Oxford University Press, 1992
7. Foreman EI, Borrill J. Long term follow-up of cognitive behavioral treatment for three cases of fear of flying. *Journal of Travel Medicine* 1994; **1**: 30–5
8. Morris HH, Estes ML. Traveler's amnesia: transient global amnesia secondary to triazolam. *Journal of the American Medical Association* 1987; **258**: 945–6
9. Modell JH. Drowning. *New England Journal of Medicine* 1993; **328**: 253–6
10. Holzer RB. Malariaprophylaxis ohne Medikamente. *Schweizerische Rundschau für Medizin Praxis* 1993; **5**: 139–43
11. Schmid RA. Personal protection against malaria, excluding chemoprophylaxis (thesis). Zürich: Universitat Zürich, 1992
12. Roland EH, Jan JE, Rigg JM. Toxic encephalopathy in a child after brief exposure to insect repellents. *Canadian Medical Association Journal* 1985; **132**: 155–6
13. Alonso PL, Lindsay SW, Armstrong SW, Armstrong JRM, *et al.* The effect of insecticide-treated bed nets on mortality of Gambian children. *Lancet* 1991; **337**: 1499–502
14. World Health Organization. *Vaccination requirements and health advice.* Geneva: WHO, 1994
15. Kozicki M, Steffen R, Schär M. 'Boil it, cook it, peel it or forget it': does this rule prevent travellers' diarrhoea? *International Journal of Epidemiology* 1985; **14**: 169–72
16. Bhopal R. Travellers' diarrhoea. *British Medical Journal* 1993; **307**: 322
17. Tjoa WS, DuPont HL, Sullivan P, *et al.* Location of food consumption and travelers' diarrhea. *American Journal of Epidemiology* 1977; **106**: 61–6

18. MacDonald KL, Cohen ML. Epidemiology of travelers' diarrhea: current perspectives. *Reviews of Infectious Diseases* 1986; **8** (Suppl 2): 117–20

19. Pennie RA, Koren G, Crevoisier C. Steady state pharmacokinetics of mefloquine in long-term travellers. *Transactions of the Royal Society of Tropical Medicine and Hygiene* 1993; **87**: 459–62

20. Lobel HO, Miani M, Eng T, Bernard KW, *et al.* Long-term malaria prophylaxis with weekly mefloquine. *Lancet* 1993; **341**: 848–51

21. Steffen R, Fuchs E, Schildknecht J, *et al.* Mefloquine compared with other malaria chemoprophylactic regimens in tourists visiting East Africa. *Lancet* 1993; **341**: 1299–303

22. Boudreau F, Schuster B, Sanchez J, *et al.* Tolerability of prophylactic Lariam® regimens. *Tropical Medicine and Parasitology* 1993; **44**: 257–65

23. Bradley D. Malaria Reference Laboratory and The Ross Institute. Prophylaxis against malaria for travellers from the United Kingdom. *British Medical Journal* 1993; **306**: 1247–52

24. Wetsteyn JC, deGeus A. Comparison of three regimens for malaria prophylaxis in travellers to east, central, and southern Africa. *British Medical Journal* 1993; **307**: 1041–3

25. Sanchez JL, DeFraites RF, Sharp TW, Hanson RK. Mefloquine or doxycycline prophylaxis in US troops in Somalia. *Lancet* 1993; **341**: 1021–2

26. Shmuklarsky MJ, Boudreau F, Pang LW, *et al.* Failure of doxycycline as a causal prophylactic agent against *Plasmodium falciparum* malaria in healthy nonimmune volunteers. *Annals of Internal Medicine* 1994; **120**: 294–9

27. Wonsgrichanalai C, Wester HK, Wimonwattrawate T, *et al.* Emergence of multidrug-resistant *Plasmodium falciparum* in Thailand: *in vitro* tracking. *American Journal of Tropical Medicine and Hygiene* 1992; **47**: 112–6

28. Suriyamongkol V, Timsaad S, Shanks GD. Mefloquine chemoprophylaxis of soldiers on the Thai Cambodian border. *Southeast Asian Journal of Tropical Medicine and Public Health* 1991; **22**: 515–8

29. Shanks GD. Drugs for prophylaxis and treatment of malaria. *Journal of Travel Medicine* 1994; **1**: 40–7

30. World Health Organization. Malaria chemoprophylaxis regimens for travellers. *Weekly Epidemiological Records* 1993; **68**: 377–83

31. Schlagenhauf P, Steffen R. Stand-by treatment of malaria in travellers: a review. *Journal of Tropical Medicine and Hygiene* 1994; **97**: 151–60

32. Farthing MJG, DuPont HL, Guandalini S, Keusch GT, Steffen R. Treatment and prevention of travellers' diarrhoea. *Gastroenterology International* 1992; **5**: 162–75

33. Oksanen PJ, Salminen S, Saxelin M, *et al.* Prevention of Travellers' Diarrhoea by *lactobacillus* GG. *Annals of Medicine* 1990; **22**: 53–56

34. Kollaritsch R, Holst H, Grobara P, Wiedermann G. Prophylaxe der Reisediarrhöe mit *Saccharomyces boulardii*. *Fortschrille der Medizin* 1993; **9**: 44–8

35. Kollaritsch H, Kremsner P, Wiedermann G, Scheiner O. Prevention of travellers' diarrhoea: comparison of different non-antibiotic preparations. *Travel Medicine International* 1989; **7**: 9–17

36. DuPont HL, Ericsson CD. Prevention and treatment of traveler's diarrhea. *New England Journal of Medicine* 1993; **328**: 1821–7
37. Steffen R, DuPont HL, Heusser R, *et al*. Prevention of traveler's diarrhea by the tablet form of bismuth subsalicylate. *Antimicrobial Agents and Chemotherapy* 1986; **29**: 625–7
38. DuPont HL, Ericsson CD, Johnson PC, Bitsura JAM, *et al*. Prevention of traveler's diarrhea by the tablet formulation of bismuth subsalicylate. *Journal of the American Medical Association* 1987; **257**: 1347–50
39. Schmid R, Schick T, Steffen R, Tschopp A, Wiik T. Comparison of seven commonly used agents for prophylaxis of seasickness. *Journal of Travel Medicine* 1994 (in press)
40. Johnson P, Hansen D, Matarazzo D, Petterson L, *et al*. Transderm Scop patches for prevention of motion sickness. *New England Journal of Medicine* 1984; **310**: 468
41. Ried LD, Carter KA, Ellsworth A. Acetazolamide or dexamethasone for prevention of acute mountain sickness: a meta-analysis. *Wilderness Medicine* 1994; **5**: 34–48
42. Bärtsch P, Maggiorini M, Ritter M, Noti C, *et al*. Prevention of high-altitude pulmonary edema by nifedipine. *New England Journal of Medicine* 1991; **325**: 1284–9
43. Steffen R, Raeber P-A. Vaccination pour les voyages internationaux. *World Health Statistics Quarterly* 1989; **42**: 85–91
44. Loutan L, Robert C-F, Raeber P-A. Outbreak of yellow fever in Kenya: how doctors got the news. *Lancet* 1993; **341**: 1030
45. Nolla-Salas J, Saballs-Radresa J. Imported yellow fever in vaccinated tourist. *Lancet* 1989; **ii**: 1275
46. Pivetaud JP, Raccurt CP, M'Bailara L, LeVigouroux A, Le Bras M. Réactions post-vaccinales à la vaccination anti-amarile. *Bulletin de la Société de Pathologie Exotique* 1986; **79**: 772–6
47. Steffen R, Kane MA, Shapiro CN, *et al*. Epidemiology and prevention of hepatitis A in travelers. *Journal of the American Medical Association* 1994 (in press)
48. Siegl G, Lemons SM. Recent advances in hepatitis A vaccine development. *Virus Research* 1990; **17**: 75–92
49. Peetermans J. Production, quality control and characterization of an inactivated hepatitis A vaccine. *Vaccine* 1992; **10**: 99–101
50. Van Damme P, Thoelen S, Cramm M, Baré H, *et al*. *Single dose inactivated hepatitis A vaccine* (Abstract). 6th International Congress for Infectious Diseases, Prague, 1994
51. Just M, Berger R. Reactogenicity and immunogenicity of inactivated hepatitis A vaccines. *Vaccine* 1992; **10**: 110–3
52. Briem H, Safary A. *Immunogenicity and safety of hepatitis A vaccine administered as a single dose with a booster at 6 months in two different age groups of adults.* (Abstract). 6th International Congress for Infectious Diseases, Prague, 1994
53. Ambrosch F, Wiedermann G, André FE. Comparison of HAV antibodies induced by vaccination, passive immunization and natural infection. In: Holinger FB, Lemon SM, Margolis HS (eds). *Viral hepatitis and liver disease*. Baltimore, MD: Williams and Wilkins, 1991: 89–100

54. Van Damme P, Thoelen S, Cramm M, Safary A, Meheus A. *Long term immunogenicity of hepatitis A vaccine* (Abstract). 6th International Congress for Infectious Diseases, Prague, 1994

55. André FE, d'Hondt ED, Delem A, Safary A. Clinical assessment and efficacy of an inactivated hepatitis A vaccine: rationale and summary of findings. *Vaccine* 1992; **10**: 160–8

56. Hughes PJ, Saadeh IK, Cox JPDT, Illis LS. Probable post-hepatitis A vaccination encephalopathy. *Lancet* 1993; **342**: 302

57. Behrens RH, Doherty JF. Severe hepatitis A despite passive immunization. *Lancet* 1993; **341**: 972

58. Stapleton JT. Passive immunization against hepatitis A. *Vaccine* 1992; **10** (Suppl 1): 45–7

59. Green MS, Cohen D, Lerman Y, *et al.* Depression of the immune response to an inactivated hepatitis A vaccine administered concomitantly with immune globulin. *Journal of Infectious Diseases* 1993; **168**: 740–3

60. Leentvaar-Kuipers A, Coutinho RA, Brulein V, Safary A. Simultaneous passive and active immunization against hepatitis A. *Vaccine* 1992; **10** (Suppl 1): 136–41

61. Studer S, Joller-Jemelka HI, Steffen R, Grob PJ. Prevalence of hepatitis A antibodies in Swiss travellers. *European Journal of Epidemiology* 1993; **9**: 50–4

62. Turner PC, Eglin RE, Woodward CG, Dave J. Screening before hepatitis A vaccination. *Lancet* 1992; **340**: 1160

63. Immunization Practices Advisory Committee. Update on Hepatitis B prevention. *Morbidity and Mortality Weekly Reports* 1987; **36**: 353–66

64. André FE. Overview of a 5 year clinical experience with a yeast-derived hepatitis B vaccine. *Vaccine* 1990; **8** (Suppl): 74–8

65. Steffen R. Risks of hepatitis B for travellers. *Vaccine* 1990; **8**: 31–2

66. Anderson LJ, Winkler WG, Hafkin B, Keenlyside RA, *et al.* Clinical experience with a human diploid cell rabies vaccine. *Journal of the American Medical Association* 1980; **244**: 781–5

67. Boe E, Nyland H. Guillain-Barré syndrome after vaccination with human diploid cell rabies vaccine. *Scandinavian Journal of Infectious Diseases* 1980; **12**: 231–2

68. Bernard KW, Fishbein DB, Miller KD. Pre-exposure rabies immunization and human diploid cell rabies vaccine: decreased antibody responses in persons immunized in developing countries. *American Journal of Tropical Medicine and Hygiene* 1985; **34**: 633–47

69. Fishbein DB, Robinson LE. Rabies. *New England Journal of Medicine* 1993; **329**: 1632–8

70. Pappaioanou M, Fishbein DB, Dreesen DW, *et al.* Antibody response to pre-exposure human diploid cell rabies vaccine given concurrently with chloroquine. *New England Journal of Medicine* 1986; **314**: 20

71. Typhoid vaccination: weighing the options (editorial). *Lancet* 1992; **340**: 341–2

72. Schwartz E, Shlim DR, Eaton M, Jenks N, Houston R, The effect of oral and parental typhoid vaccination on the rate of infection with *Salmonella typhi* and *Salmonella paratyphi A* among foreigners in Nepal. *Archives of Internal Medicine* 1990; **150**: 349–51

73. Hirschel B, Wütkrich R, Somaini B, Steffen R. Inefficacy of the commercial live oral Ty21a vaccine in the prevention of typhoid fever. *European Journal of Clinical Microbiology* 1985; **4**: 295–8
74. Ambrosch F, Hirschl A, Kollaritsch H, Kremsner P, *et al. Immunologic investigations with oral live typhoid vaccine Ty21a strain.* In: Steffen R, Lobel HO, Haworth J, Bradley DJ (eds). Proceedings of the first conference on international travel medicine, Heidelberg: Springer, 1989: 248–53
75. Gold JA, Sibbald RG, Phillips MJ, Edwards V. Angioimmunoblastic lymphadenopathy following typhoid AB vaccination and terminating in disseminated infection. *Archives of Pathology Laboratory Medicine* 1985; **109**: 1085–9
76. Pounder DJ. Sudden, unexpected death following typhoid cholera vaccination. *Forensic Science International* 1984; **24**: 95–8
77. Moser MR, Bendor TR, Margolis HS, Noble GR, *et al.* An outbreak of influenza aboard a commercial airliner. *American Journal of Epidemiology* 1979; **110**: 1–6
78. Herzog C. Meningokokkeninfektionen: Impf- und Chemoprophylaxe *Therapeutische Umschau* 1983: **40**: 239–43
79. Koch S, Steffen R. Meningococcal disease in travelers: vaccination recommendations. *Journal of Travel Medicine* 1994; **1**: 4–7
80. Centers for Disease Control and Prevention. *Inactivated Japanese encephalitis virus vaccine: recommendations of the Advisory Committee on Immunization Practices.* Atlanta, GA: *Morbidity and Mortality Weekly Report* 1993, no. RR-1
81. World Health Organization. Japanese encephalitis: inactivated Japanese encephalitis virus vaccine. *Weekly Epidemiological Records* 1994; **69**: 113–20
82. Hoke CH, Nisalak A, Sangawhipa N, *et al.* Protection against Japanese encephalitis by inactivated vaccines. *New England Journal of Medicine* 1988; **319**: 608–14
83. Ruff TA, Eisen D, Fuller A. Adverse reactions to Japanese encephalitis vaccine. *Lancet* 1991; **338**: 881–2
84. Wittlinger F, Steffen R, Watanabe H, Handszuh H. Travellers' cholera: underestimated, but does it matter? *Journal of Travel Medicine* 1994; (in press)
85. Fourteen IATA member airlines. *Travel Information Manual*, Boekhoven-Bosch, Utrecht (published monthly)
86. Gotuzzo E, Burton B, Sas C, *et al.* Safety, immunogenicity, and excretion pattern of single-dose live oral cholera vaccine CVD 103-HgR in Peruvian adults of high and low socioeconomic levels. *Infection and Immunology* 1993; **61**: 3994–7
87. Levine MM, Kaper JB. Live oral vaccines against cholera: an update. *Vaccine* 1993; **11**: 207–12
88. Goerre S, Kesselring J, Hartmann K, Kuhn M, Reinhart WH. Neurologische Nebenwirkungen nach Impfung gegen die Frühsommer Meningo-Enzephalitis. *Schweizerische Medizinische Wochenschrift* 1993; **123**: 654–7
89. Gold R, Wiethölter H, Rihs I, Löwer J, Kappos L. Frühsommer-Meningoenzephalitis Impfung. *Deutsche Medizinische Wochenschrift* 1992; **117**: 112–6

90. Colditz GA, Brewer TF, Berkey CS, *et al.* Efficacy of BCG vaccine in the prevention of tuberculosis. *Journal of the American Medical Association* 1994; **271**: 698–702

91. Barnet ED, Klein JO. Pneumococcal vaccination for travel to Spain. *Lancet* 1992; **340**: 681

92. van Zwanenberg D. The last epidemic of plague in England? Suffolk 1906–1918. *Medical History* 1970; **14**: 63–74

93. European Community Directive. *Communicable Disease Report CDR Weekly* 1993; 3

94. Behrens RH, Roberts JA. Is travel prophylaxis worthwhile? Economic appraisal of prophylactic measures against malaria, hepatitis A, and typhoid in travellers. *British Medical Journal* 1994; **309**: 918–22

12 | Economic aspects of travel health

Rodney Y Cartwright
Consultant Microbiologist and Director, Public Health Laboratory, Guildford

Tourism is a rapidly developing international economic force. According to the World Tourism Organisation, the numbers increase annually, as does the value of receipts associated with tourism. In 1950 there were 25,282,000 international arrivals, accounting for US\$ 2,100 million in receipts (excluding international fare receipts). By 1980, these figures had risen to 287,771,000 arrivals and US\$ 102,008 million, and in 1992, to 475,580,000 arrivals and US\$ 278,705 million (Table 1 and Fig 1). It has been estimated that by the turn of the century tourism will be the major global economic force, having overtaken the oil and automobile industries to occupy the prime position.[1]

Areas of the world visited continue to grow, with the greatest comparative increase in east Asia, the Pacific region and Africa.

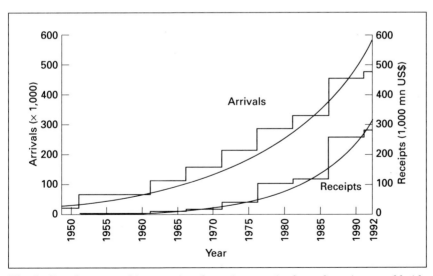

Fig 1. *Development of international tourism: arrivals and receipts worldwide (excluding international fare receipts). Actual figures and exponential curve fit.* Data Source: World Tourism Organisation, 1993.

Table 1. Development of international tourism: raw data on arrivals and receipts 1950–92

Year	Arrivals (mn)	Receipts (1,000 mn US$)
1950	25	2
1960	69	7
1965	113	12
1970	160	18
1975	214	41
1980	288	102
1985	330	115
1990	456	255
1992	476	279

Tourists are exposed to a variety of health hazards, which have health consequences for the individual and may also affect the health of a community in medical and economic terms.

The prime aim of the tourist industry is to generate money. This is best achieved when the tourist is satisfied with the product and suffers no ill effect from whatever cause. The dissatisfied and unhealthy tourist increases the claims for compensation and reduces the likelihood of repeat bookings to a resort or with a particular operator. The cost of ill health does not fall directly on the tourist industry, but the consequences may have a severe economic impact. It is, therefore, to the benefit of all concerned to reduce to a minimum health risks in tourists.

The health of tourists is usually closely linked to the health of the indigenous population in tourist areas and to the quality of the local infrastructure. Well developed areas, with good roads, safe water and sewage systems, high awareness of hygiene and safety, and good medical services have lower reported health problems among tourists compared to underdeveloped areas. This applies not only to communicable diseases (especially travellers' diarrhoea) but also to accidents.

An increasing number of tourists wish to visit 'third world' countries while enjoying 'first world' facilities and standards. This is an impossible objective—although many of the former have high quality hotels and a superficial appearance of high standards, the services on which they depend may be woefully inadequate. It is in the interests of those concerned both with the economics of tourism and with the health of the tourist to work together to safe-guard the latter. Prevention of illness and accidents is an essential prerequisite for the smooth growth of tourism. Adverse health episodes not only affect the individual tourist but may, as a conse-quence of press reports, result in a reduction in the number of tourists visiting a region or resort, with a resultant effect on the economic health of a local holiday community and the tourist industry generally.

In spite of good intentions — and not infrequently appropriate legislation — tourism development is usually well ahead of infra-structure provision, which is regarded as essential for public health in the major 'sending' (home) country of the tourist. Inadequate water supply and sewage disposal systems are probably the main factors responsible for travellers' diarrhoea (Chapter 3), the com-monest travel-associated illness. Poor roads are an important contributory factor in road accidents (Chapter 6).

Health risks associated with tourist areas have been identified, but there is a lack of adequate epidemiological surveillance which would provide a quantifiable measure of illness. For example, it is known anecdotally that most tourists travelling along the river Nile suffer a gastrointestinal disturbance, but the true incidence is not known, the causative factors are unidentified, and the cost-effec-tiveness of control measures unassessed. There is an urgent need for adequately funded research to enable effective control programmes to be developed.

Major improvements in infrastructure require the use of national — and often international — funding, the financial balance being achieved through tourism earnings. Tourism is the major source of foreign earnings in many countries; it is therefore an essential aspect of the national economy. An important consequence of tourist health improvement programmes is that the health of the indigenous population will also be improved — of significance when politicians are debating national expenditure programmes. A healthy tourist industry can provide income to fund other political-ly desirable programmes, so it is necessary to protect the income source by actively improving the health and safety of tourists. In addition, supranational groups such as the European Community and the non-governmental organisations, the World Health Organization and the World Tourism Organisation, all have active programmes to support health and safety in tourism.

Various aspects of the economics of health and tourism, the role(s) of the tourist, the 'sending' and 'receiving' countries, and the tourist industry will be examined in this chapter.

The examples and discussion which follow will be related primarily to leisure tourism and travel, with a particular emphasis on
package travel. Appropriate preparation of the traveller, provision
of an adequate infrastructure (and the consequences of failure)
also apply, although at times in differing ways, to the business
traveller and the individual tourist.

The tourist

The individual tourist's decision on a destination for a holiday will
be influenced by many factors, with the cost of the trip playing a
large part. Health considerations will usually have a low priority,
although any adverse publicity for the preferred areas will be a
negative factor. The tourist will invariably assume that any accommodation listed in a brochure will be 'safe'. The brochure may
contain advice to the intending traveller indicating that medical
advice should be sought before going on holiday, but the tour
operator is required by law to provide information only on health
formalities,[2] which in effect means information on countries where
yellow fever vaccination is required before entry (Chapter 11). The
tour operator and travel agent will, however, encourage tourists to
buy travel insurance to provide cover for medical or repatriation
expenses in the event of a holiday-acquired illness or accident. Sale
of travel insurance is an income generating activity for the travel
agent — but it is always recommended too because the costs of an
accident or illness may be financially crippling for the individual
tourist.

The wise tourist will spend money on health protection before
going on holiday. In preparation for travel, the tourist may visit his
or her general practitioner (GP) or alternatively, a travel clinic.
Some clinics will charge a fee just for advice. Mosquito repellents,
oral rehydration salts, anti-diarrhoeal medication, and travel kits
for use in areas with a high incidence of HIV and AIDS, may all be
recommended (for purchasing) to the traveller. If immunisations
and vaccinations are required, they may be available through the
National Health Service (NHS) but they incur a prescription
charge. Yellow fever immunisation and the accompanying certificate can be obtained only from a recognised centre; the full cost is
borne by the traveller.

The cost of health precautions whilst on holiday must also be
included in the travel budget. If, for example, the water supply is
suspect, it is important to buy bottled water. Food from street
traders may be tempting and considerably cheaper than that in

restaurants, but the health risks are much greater and it should be avoided. Transportation safety is important, but standards are frequently inadequate or even entirely ignored; cars with working seat belts may, for example, be more expensive to hire but may save a life.

For a tourist who is not insured, medical attention can be expensive, and repatriation or specialised care difficult to obtain. NHS provisions cannot be translocated to holiday countries; proof of ability to pay costs is frequently a prerequisite for treatment.

The home country

The governments of many home countries recognise that they have an important role relating to the health of their population travelling abroad. Part of the health budget should be allocated, so that relevant pre-travel advice is readily available. GPs and travel clinics may advise the traveller — but what is the quality of the information they provide, and where or whom are their sources? The Department of Health (DoH) has for some years produced an advice booklet (T4) for travellers; it is currently producing a book for the medical profession on health advice for overseas travel. This book will have a yellow cover, and complement the green-covered book on immunisation. Posters and leaflets on specific illnesses such as AIDS, rabies and malaria are also produced.

The availability of some vaccines on an NHS prescription and the provision of item-for-services to GPs is a matter of considerable confusion and debate. Should the taxpayer support the health protection of an intending traveller or should the entire cost be borne by the latter?

The epidemiological surveillance provided by the Communicable Disease Surveillance Centre (CDSC) of the Public Health Laboratory Service in England and Wales and by the Communicable Disease Unit (Scotland) is financed by public monies. The information obtained is essential for the DoH in formulating advice to the medical profession, travel clinics, and to travellers.

The economic impact on the home country resulting from the medical and social services costs of the traveller returning ill or becoming ill after return (with a travel-acquired illness) may be considerable. Primary care and hospital services may be required as well as social security payments. Public health resources may be necessary to control the spread of some imported communicable diseases. For example, in the last six months of 1993, 87 cases of legionnaires' disease were reported to the European working group on

Legionella spp infections in travellers who had visited other countries. Many of these patients required intensive and expensive in-patient hospital care, and seven are known to have died.[3]

Reliable costings of travel-associated infections are not available, but it must be recognised that the economic impact on the home country is by no means inconsiderable. A study on the economics of salmonellosis in 1988 and 1989 concluded that the average cost associated with a *Salmonella* spp infection was £789 overall.[4] In 1992, 495 gastrointestinal infections were reported to CDSC in travellers returning from Kenya. Only 180 of these were caused by *Salmonella* spp, but it is likely that the economic impact of the other infections was similar (Table 2). On 1988–89 prices, the cost of these infections totalled nearly £440,000. There would have been many other unreported cases which nevertheless incurred some costs. Although the true figure is unknown, an estimate of 10% actual reporting is often used; this would raise the above cost to the order of £5 million.

The impact on public health resources is exemplified by five outbreaks involving over 140 persons suffering from *Shigella sonnei* dysentery linked to index cases returning from Albuferia, Portugal during 1984. All these outbreaks were investigated by environmental health officers and medical officers of environmental health, and involved the processing of numerous faecal specimens and subsequent typing of the *S. sonnei* isolates.

Who should pay for the health care and social security payments of travellers who return with an illness acquired abroad — the general taxpayer or the traveller?

Table 2. Gastrointestinal infections reported to the Communicable Disease Surveillance Centre in travellers returning from Kenya in 1992

Infection	No. cases
Salmonella spp	180
Campylobacter jejuni	143
Shigella spp	68
Giardia lamblia	42
Vibrio spp	20
Entamoeba histolytica	18
Aeromonas spp	13
Cryptosporidium parvum	6
Blastocystis hominis	5
Total	495

The holiday country

The holiday country has perhaps the most both to gain and to lose in economic terms when an area becomes subjected to ill health among its tourists. Many holiday countries rely heavily on tourism as their main source of foreign income, and the total economy of some holiday towns may depend on tourism receipts. A downturn in tourism will have repercussions throughout a community, and affect not only those directly involved with the tourist but also those providing supplies and support.

An essential prerequisite for successful tourism is a high quality public health infrastructure for the total community. It is not sufficient to provide a good potable water supply and safe sewage disposal to individual hotels whilst the local inhabitants obtain their untreated water from rivers and lorries and have open sewage channels. It is these local inhabitants who are the kitchen workers and food handlers in the hotels and restaurants. A gastrointestinal illness in a food handler is a well recognised hazard.

Water supply

A safe potable water supply of adequate quality is probably the most important measure to safeguard tourist health. Water treatment plants need to be built, also service reservoirs and water distribution networks sufficient for the indigenous population and the tourists — both now and in the foreseeable future; they must be easy to maintain and have adequate fail-safe mechanisms. Chlorination methods in many holiday areas are primitive and do not provide consistent levels of chlorine. Modern systems are expensive to install and maintain, but they make long-term economic and health sense. In the absence of safe tap-water, properly controlled bottled water should be available.

There has been considerable debate on the safety of bathing waters — especially the sea at popular holiday coastal areas. Untreated or partially treated sewage may be pumped into the sea along short sea outfalls, with a consequently unacceptable level of sewage-indicator organisms in the bathing waters. The EC directive on bathing water[5] is being revised. The consultation paper indicates that failure to meet standards would result in bathing waters being closed to the public; this would damage local tourism, but be of benefit for the health of both the local people and the tourists.

Many countries have identified national funds or obtained loans from the International Monetary Fund or the World Bank to improve both potable water supply and sewage disposal systems.

Food hygiene

Food hygiene is of major importance — especially the training and inspection of food handlers. The EC directive on the hygiene of foodstuffs[6] provides a framework for legislation which, when enacted, will necessitate increased expenditure by most countries. Implementation of the directive should improve food hygiene for both the indigenous population and the tourist. It should be remembered, however, that tourists are likely to eat meals in hotels and restaurants. Hygiene inspections are important, but inspectors need to be paid a salary at a sufficient level to reduce the possibility of bribery by hotel and restaurant managers (personal experience confirms that this is a not uncommon practice in some tourist areas).

Holiday countries may also experience conflicting interests between government departments. In some countries, hoteliers are actively discouraged from using electricity or fuel oil to heat water during the summer months, heating depending on solar panels. The problem here is that the water temperature may not be high enough to control the multiplication of *Legionella* spp in the water system (an economic versus a health argument).

The impact on local medical services of illness among the tourists may be considerable; in many holiday areas this has been met by the development of private hospitals and clinics. Ill tourists, however, are an important source of income for many medical practitioners who may not be particularly willing to co-operate in the reduction of travel-associated illness.

In common with the home country, there is a general lack of information on both the extent of illness among tourists and the true economic impact on the community. This makes a cost-effective assessment of any 'improvements' very difficult.

The tourist industry

Travel agents, tour operators, transport operators, hoteliers and restauranteurs are all part of the tourism industry, which aims to provide an enjoyable and safe product for its clients. They are all in business to make a profit, and must therefore promote the positive aspects of their product whilst ensuring that clients are adequately warned and/or protected. The dividing line between requirements and the wishes of the health profession and financial controllers is narrow, with frequent misunderstandings regarding each other's position. Major tour operators accept that there is a fine balance: it was estimated that UK tour operators paid £8–9 million in compensation for illness and injury in 1992.

Reliance on hotel standards has depended on acceptance of local certificates of hygiene and safety, which it is now recognised may be misleading. The EC 'package holiday' directive[2] places a legal onus on the tour operator for all aspects of the package, including those provided by a third party. This is encouraging the International Federation of Tour Operators to produce health and safety guidelines for inspecting hotels; these will, however, need to be totally objective as inspections will be carried out by contractors with no health or hygiene training.

The tour operators are probably the most powerful lobby within the industry for the promotion of improved standards. They also have the most comprehensive collection of data on illness in tourists. These data are used to encourage countries, local authorities and hoteliers to develop active health and hygiene programmes. If made freely available, this information could have adverse effects on tour operator's programmes — forcing them to withdraw from resorts. If this happens, a competitor who may not be concerned with long-term improvements may move in. Short-term risks, yet long-term improvements represents a delicate balance between travel health and economics.

Individual hoteliers vary in their response to requests for hygiene and safety improvements. Large chains usually recognise the importance of high standards and have their own internal quality control programmes. Smaller hoteliers, however, may be loath to invest money in improvements, especially if operators continue to contract beds. In popular areas, if one operator withdraws there are usually several others waiting to take up the contract.

Thomson Tour Operators Ltd have for many years recognised the importance of reliable and on-going information for the health of their clients, and have paid for the inclusion of a health question in their 'client satisfaction' questionnaire. This provides data on about one million clients annually. As a result, resorts with an exceptionally high incidence of illness, in particular travellers' diarrhoea (defined as 'any symptom of possible gastroenteritis' reported by the client), have been identified. The company has in turn encouraged governments, local authorities and hoteliers to investigate and take remedial action when necessary.[7]

The economical consequence(s) of failure

If preventive measures fail and illness results, economic consequences may affect not only the individual tourist but also the home country, the holiday country, and the tourist industry in general.

The outbreak of typhoid fever at Salou, Spain, in 1989 exemplifies some of the economic aspects of health problems among tourists. Surveillance of British tourists at the resort in the 1986, 1987 and 1988 summer seasons indicated levels of 'subjective' travellers' diarrhoea which peaked to over 20% each year, whereas nearby resorts had levels not exceeding 10%. Tour operators had notified the local authorities of their concern, and were reassured that various public health measures were being taken. In 1989, increased levels were observed earlier in the season. The illness had all the classical features of travellers' diarrhoea but the local authorities were not unduly concerned. Some tourists required hospital admission for rehydration. In July, cases of *Salmonella typhi* infection spread throughout the town — affecting both tourists and the indigenous population. Fourteen cases were identified, seven in British tourists. A major investigation by the Catalan Health Department indicated water to be the possible source. The tap-water in the town was adequately chlorinated, but undrinkable because of its high salt content (the source wells have very low water levels). Hotels were purchasing untreated water from tankers filled at an inland river site. Three different strains were subsequently recognised (distinguished by bacteriophage typing at the laboratory of Enteric Pathogens, Central Public Health Laboratory, London). It was fortuitous that a new water supply providing safe water became operational within a few weeks of the outbreak; there were no further cases, and the incidence of travellers' diarrhoea fell dramatically; it has continued at a level below 10%.

The impact of this outbreak on tourism was dramatic, with immediate cancellations and a reduction in the number of tourists in subsequent years. In 1988 air inclusive tours from the UK to Salou had reached 120,000; these fell to 80,000 in 1989 and 20–30,000 in 1990, 1991 and 1992 (Fig 2). There were numerous consequences of this outbreak:

- the infected tourists had to pay medical expenses and suffered loss of earnings;
- the insurance companies paid out on policies;
- the UK health service investigated and treated cases and provided extra advice to travellers;
- the Spanish authorities had to launch a major public health investigation, in addition to paying local medical expenses;
- the economy of the area suffered a major reduction in foreign income; and

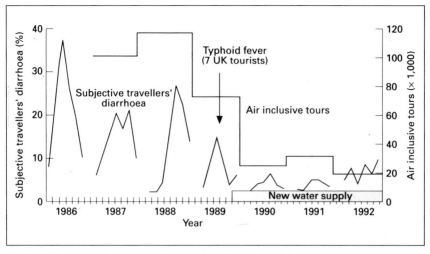

Fig 2. *The economic impact of an outbreak of typhoid fever in Salou, Spain, and the effect of a new potable water supply on the incidence of subjective travellers' diarrhoea.* Data Source: Thomson Tour Operations Ltd.

- tour operators were required to make alternative arrangements for many clients, and their Salou programme suffered a major set back.

It is fortunate that a new water supply had been completed, but earlier action to provide safe water should have prevented the fourteen cases of *S. typhi* infection and the subsequent economic consequences.

Summary

Economics, health and travel are closely interlinked. Investment in tourism should always include attention to public health infrastructure, health and hygiene. Tourists should be well prepared before visiting a foreign country, and health precautions always included in their budget.

Failure to safeguard the health of tourists has important economic consequences for the tourist, the home country, the holiday country and the tourist industry itself. There is an urgent need to improve epidemiological surveillance of illness, develop risk assessment models, and to undertake economic appraisals of preventive strategies.

Prevention of illness in tourists makes medical, tourism and economic sense — but, all too often, there is no provision for funding preventive programmes.

References

1. *Global tourism forecasts to the year 2000 and beyond — executive summary.* Madrid: World Tourism Organisation, 1993: 20
2. Council Directive. Package travel, package holidays and package tours (90/134/EEC). *Official Journal of the European Communities* 1990; **158**: 59–64
3. European surveillance of legionnaires' disease associated with travel. *Communicable Disease Report Weekly* 1994; **4**: 25
4. Sockett PN, Roberts JA. The social and economic impact of salmonellosis. *Epidemiology and Infection* 1991; **107**: 335–7
5. Council Directive. The quality of bathing water (76/160/EEC) *Official Journal of the European Communities* 1976; L31/1–7
6. Council Directive. The hygiene of foodstuffs (93/43/EEC) *Official Journal of the European Communities* 1993;L175/1–11
7. Cartwright RY. Epidemiology of travellers' diarrhoea in British package holiday tourists. *Public Health Laboratory Service Microbiology Digest* 1992; **9**: 365–70

13 | Prevention of viral hepatitis*

Arie J Zuckerman
Dean and Professor of Medical Microbiology,
Royal Free Hospital School of Medicine, London

Prevention and control of hepatitis A

In areas of high prevalence of hepatitis A virus (HAV) infection most children have antibodies to HAV virus by the age of three, and such infections are generally asymptomatic. Infections acquired later in life are of increasing clinical severity. Less than 10% of cases of acute HAV infection in children up to age six are icteric, increasing to 40–50% in the 6–14 age group, and 70–80% in adults. Only 9% of the 115,551 cases of HAV infection in the USA between 1983 and 1987, but more than 70% of the fatalities, were in those aged over 49 years. It is important, therefore, to protect those at risk following personal contact with infected individuals or who travel to highly endemic areas. Other groups at risk of HAV infection include:

- staff and residents of institutions for the mentally handicapped, and day care centres for children;
- sexually active male homosexuals;
- narcotic drug abusers;
- sewage workers;
- certain groups of health care workers (particularly those seconded for work overseas);
- medical students on elective studies abroad;
- military personnel; and
- certain low socio-economic groups in defined community settings.

In some developing countries, the incidence of clinical HAV infection is increasing because improvements in socio-economic conditions mean that infection occurs later in life. Strategies for immunisation against HAV are yet to be developed and agreed.

Passive immunisation

Control of HAV is difficult (see also Chapters 9 and 11). Faecal shedding of the virus is highest during the late incubation period

---

*Royal College of Physicians lecture delivered on 22 June 1994

and prodromal phase of the illness; therefore, strict isolation is not a useful control measure. Spread of HAV is reduced by simple hygienic measures and the sanitary disposal of excreta.

Normal human immunoglobulin (IG), containing at least 100 IU/ml of anti-HAV antibody, given intramuscularly before exposure to the virus or early during the incubation period, will prevent or attenuate clinical illness. The dose should be at least 2 IU of anti-HAV antibody/kg body weight, but in special cases (eg pregnancy and patients with liver disease) the dosage may be doubled. IG does not always prevent infection and excretion of HAV, and inapparent or subclinical hepatitis may ensue. The efficacy of passive immunisation is based on the presence of HAV antibody in the IG, and the minimum titre of antibody required for protection is believed to be 5–10 IU/ml. IG is used most commonly for close personal contacts of patients with HAV and for those exposed to contaminated food. It has also been used effectively for controlling outbreaks in institutions such as homes for the mentally handicapped and nursery schools.

Prophylaxis with IG is recommended for persons without HAV antibody visiting highly endemic areas. IG administration to travellers should be repeated after six months unless it has been demonstrated that the recipient has developed HAV antibodies.

Killed hepatitis A vaccines

The foundations for an HAV vaccine were laid in 1975 by Provost and Hilleman[1] who demonstrated that formalin-inactivated virus extracted from the liver of infected marmosets induced protective antibodies in susceptible animals on challenge with live virus. In the following year,[2] after serial passage in marmosets, they cultivated HAV in a cloned line of fetal rhesus monkey kidney cells (FRhK6) — thereby opening the way for the production of HAV vaccines.

Several groups subsequently demonstrated that prior adaptation in marmosets is not a prerequisite to growth of the virus in cell cultures. Various strains of virus have now been isolated directly from clinical material using several cell lines (including human diploid fibroblasts) and various techniques employed to increase the yield of virus in cell culture. Safety and immunogenicity studies of HAV vaccines using several different adapted strains of virus with an adjuvant have now been completed, and a vaccine using the CR326 and HM175 strains has been licensed in many countries. Other preparations are undergoing clinical trial.

Live attenuated hepatitis A vaccines

The major advantage of live attenuated vaccines (eg, the Sabin type of oral poliomyelitis vaccine) include:

- ease of large-scale administration by the oral route;
- relatively low cost, since the virus vaccine strain replicates in the gut;
- production of both local immunity in the intestine and humoral immunity — thereby mimicking infection; and
- longer-term protection.

Disadvantages include:

- potential of reversion towards virulence;
- interference with the vaccine strain by other intraluminal intestinal viruses;
- relative instability of the vaccine; and
- shedding of the virus strain in the faeces for prolonged periods.

The most extensively reported studies on live attenuated HAV vaccines are based on the CR326 and HM175 strains of the virus attenuated by prolonged passage in cell culture.

Two variants of the CR326 strain have been investigated in FRhK6, MRC5 and WI-38 cells after passage in marmoset liver. Inoculation of susceptible marmosets demonstrated seroconversion, and protection on challenge. Biochemical evidence of liver damage did not occur in susceptible chimpanzees, although some had histological evidence of mild hepatitis with the F variant, and the vaccine virus was shed in the faeces for about 12 weeks prior to seroconversion. There was no evidence of reversion towards virulence. Studies in human volunteers indicated incomplete attenuation of the F variant, but better results were obtained with the F1 variant and liver enzymes were not elevated.[3]

Studies with the HM175 strain, isolated and passaged in African green monkey kidney cells, showed that it was not fully attenuated for marmosets, although it did not induce liver damage on challenge. Further passage and adaptation of HM175 revealed some evidence of virus replication in the liver of chimpanzees and minimal shedding of the virus into faeces.

Other studies are in progress. A live attenuated HAV vaccine is being used in the People's Republic of China.

As with vaccine strains of poliovirus(es), attenuation may be associated with mutations in the 5' non-coding region of the genome which affect secondary structure. There is also evidence that mutations in the region of the genome encoding the nonstructural polypeptides may be important for adaptation to cell culture and attenuation.

Prevention and control of hepatitis B

Passive immunisation

Hepatitis B (HBIG) is prepared from pooled plasma with a high titre of HBV surface antibody, and may confer temporary passive immunity in certain defined conditions. The major indication for its administration is a single acute exposure to HBV, such as occurs when blood containing HBV surface antigen (HBsAg) is inoculated, ingested or splashed on to mucous membranes and conjunctiva. The optimal dose has not been established, but ones in the range of 200–500 IU have been used effectively. It should be administered as early as possible after exposure, and preferably within 48 hours (never more than seven days following exposure). The dose in adults is usually 3 ml (containing 200 IU of anti-surface antibody (anti-HBs) per ml). The general recommendation is two doses of HBIG administered 30 days apart.

Results using HBIG for prophylaxis in babies at risk of infection with HBV are encouraging if given as soon as possible, and within 12 hours of birth; the chance of the baby developing the persistent carrier state is thereby reduced by about 70%. Recent studies using combined passive and active immunisation indicate an efficacy approaching 90%. The dose of HBIG recommended in the newborn is 1–2 ml (200 IU of anti-HBs per ml).

Active immunisation

Immunisation against HBV is required for groups at increased risk of acquiring this infection (see also Chapter 11). These groups include:

- Patients who require repeated transfusions of blood or blood products, prolonged inpatient treatment, have frequent tissue penetration or repeated access to the circulation, and those with natural or acquired immune deficiency or malignant disease.
- Health care personnel and the staff of institutions for the mentally handicapped and some semi-closed institutions, in whom viral hepatitis is an occupational hazard.
- Intravenous drug abusers, sexually active male homosexuals, prostitutes and others who frequently change sexual partners, in whom there are high rates of HBV infection.

- Individuals working in highly endemic areas — who are also at increased risk of infection.
- Women in areas of the world where the 'carrier state' is high — in view of the increased risk of transmission of infection to their offspring.
- Young infants, children and susceptible individuals living in certain tropical and subtropical areas where present socio-economic conditions are poor and the prevalence of HBV high.

Failure to grow HBV in tissue culture has directed attention to the use of other preparations for active immunisation. Immunisation with HBsAg leads to the production of protective surface antibody. Purified 22-mm spherical surface antigen particles have been developed as vaccines; they have been prepared from the plasma of asymptomatic carriers. Studies on protective efficacy in high-risk groups have demonstrated both the value of these vaccines, and also their safety. There is no risk of transmission of AIDS or any other infection by vaccines derived from plasma which meet the World Health Organization (WHO) requirements of 1981, 1983 and 1987. Local reactions reported after immunisation have been minor, and occur in less than 20% of immunised individuals. Temperature elevations up to 38°C have been observed in a few individuals only.

Site of vaccination injection

HBV vaccination should be given in the upper arm or anterolateral aspect of the thigh, and not the buttock. There are over 100 reports of unexpectedly low antibody seroconversion rates after HBV immunisation using injection into the buttock. In one centre in the USA, a low antibody response was noted in 54% of healthy adult health care personnel. Many studies have since shown that antibody response rate is significantly higher in centres using deltoid injection than in centres using the buttock. On the basis of antibody tests after vaccination, the Advisory Committee on Immunization Practices of the Centers of Disease Control, USA, recommended that the arm be used as the site for HBV vaccination in adults; this is also advised by the UK Department of Health.

A comprehensive study by Shaw *et al.*[4] showed that participants who received the vaccine in the deltoid had antibody titres up to 17 times higher than those who received the injections into the buttock. Furthermore, the latter were 2–4 times more likely to fail to mount a minimum antibody level of 10 mIU/ml following vaccination. (Recent reports have also implicated buttock injection as a possible factor in failure of rabies post-exposure prophylaxis using a human diploid cell rabies vaccine.[5])

Factors responsible for this failure may include:

- needles shorter than 5 cm are likely to inject vaccine into deep fat in the buttock — where there is a lack of phagocytic and antigen-presenting cells;
- the delay with which antigen becomes available to the circulation after deposition in fat leads to a delay in processing by macrophages and eventually presentation to T and B cells; and possibly
- the denaturation (by enzymes) of any antigen which has remained in fat for hours or days.

The importance of these factors is supported by the finding that thicker skinfold is associated with a lowered antibody response.[6]

These observations have important public health implications — well illustrated by the estimate that about 20% (60,000) of subjects immunised against HBV via the buttock in the USA by March 1985 had failed to attain a minimum antibody level of 10 mIU/ml, and were therefore not protected. Recommended anti-HBs titres for protection range from 50–100 mIU/ml.

HBV surface antibody titres should be measured in all individuals who have been immunised against HBV by injection into the buttock. When this is not possible, a complete course of three injections of vaccine should be administered into either the deltoid muscle or the anterolateral aspect of the thigh, now known to be the only acceptable sites for HBV immunisation.[7]

Indications for immunisation against hepatitis B

Current indications for the use of HBV vaccines in the UK — a low prevalence area — are summarised below (although these recommendations may have to be revised). Recommendations for immunisation in intermediate and high prevalence regions also include universal immunisation of infants.[8,9] Many countries, including the USA and Italy (low prevalence areas), introduced universal immunisation for infants in 1992, and it is expected that most European countries, and some others, will implement this policy by 1996.

Current UK policy on immunisation against hepatitis B

1. *Health care personnel:*

   All health care personnel in frequent contact with blood or needles (including medical, dental, nursing and midwifery students). Groups at highest risk include:

- personnel (including teaching and training staff) directly involved over a period of time in patient care in residential institutions for the mentally handicapped, where there is a known high risk of hepatitis;
- personnel directly involved in patient care over a period of time, working in units giving treatment to individuals with a known high risk of HBV infection;
- personnel directly involved in patient care working in haemodialysis, haemophilia and other centres performing regular maintenance treatment with blood or blood products;
- laboratory workers regularly exposed to increased risk from infected material;
- personnel seconded to work in geographical areas of the world with a high prevalence of HBV infection — if they are to be directly involved in patient care; and
- dentists, dental students and ancillary dental personnel with direct patient contact.

2. *Patients:*

- on first entry into a residential institution for the mentally handicapped where there is a known high incidence of HBV infection;
- treated by maintenance haemodialysis;
- undergoing major surgery who are likely to require a large number of blood transfusions and/or treatment with blood products.

3. *Contacts of patients with HBV:*

- spouses and other sexual contacts of patients with acute HBV infection or carriers of HBV, and other family members in close contact.

4. *Other indications:*

- infants born to mothers who are persistent carriers of HBsAg or have become HBsAg-positive as a result of recent infection, particularly if hepatitis *e* antigen (HBeAg) is detectable, and HBV-positive mothers who are anti-HBe. The optimum timing for IG to be given at a contralateral site is either at birth or within 12 hours thereafter;
- health care workers accidentally pricked with a needle used for patients with HBV infection. The vaccine may be used alone, or in combination with HBIG as an alternative to

passive immunisation with HBIG alone. Studies of the efficacy of these different immunisation schedules are nearing completion.

5. *Immediate protection:*

Immediate protection is required, for example, for infants born to carrier or HBsAg-positive mothers, or after accidental inoculation. Active immunisation with the vaccine should be combined with simultaneous administration of HBIG at a different site. Passive immunisation with up to 3 ml (200 IU anti-HBs per ml) of HBIG has been shown not to interfere with an active immune response. A single dose of HBIG (usually 3 ml for adults, 1–2 ml for the newborn) is sufficient for healthy individuals. If infection has already occurred at the time of the first immunisation, virus replication is unlikely to be inhibited completely, but severe illness and, most importantly, development of the HBV carrier state may be prevented in many individuals, particularly infants born to carrier mothers.

6. *Immunocompromised patients and the elderly:*

Immune response to current HBV vaccines is poorer in immunocompromised patients and the elderly. For example, only about 60% of patients undergoing treatment by maintenance haemodialysis develop anti-HBs. It is therefore suggested that patients with chronic renal damage should be immunised as soon as it appears likely that they will ultimately require maintenance haemodialysis and/or renal transplantation. Consideration should be given to the use of blood from healthy immunised donors with a high anti-HBs titre for routine haemodialysis of patients who respond poorly to immunisation against HBV.

7. *Other groups* at risk of HBV infection include the following:
   - individuals who frequently change sexual partners — especially sexually active male homosexuals and prostitutes;
   - intravenous drug abusers;
   - staff at reception centres for refugees and immigrants from areas of the world where HBV infection is very common, for example, south-east Asia;
   - although at 'lower risk', consideration should also be given to long-term prisoners and staff of custodial institutions, ambulance and rescue services, and selected police personnel;
   - military personnel are included in some countries.

Developing new hepatitis B immunisation strategies

There is now strong support for the introduction of universal ante-natal screening to identify HBV carrier mothers and to vaccinate their babies. It is important that any new strategy does not interfere with the delivery of vaccine to this group — immunisation of them will have the greatest impact in reducing the number of new HBV carriers. It is difficult to estimate the life-time risk of acquiring a hepatitis infection for children outside this group.

There are four main approaches to immunisation strategies:

1. To continue vaccination of 'high risk' babies, as defined above.
2. Universal adolescent immunisation.
3. Infant immunisation.
4. Universal vaccination.

Vaccination of adolescents

Vaccinating adolescents would deliver immunisation close to the time when 'risk behaviour' exposes them to infection. It could be delivered as part of a wider package on health education in general, to include:

- sex education;
- risk of AIDS;
- dangers of drug abuse and of smoking; and
- benefits of a healthy diet and lifestyle.

The problems of this approach are:

- persuading parents to accept vaccination of their children against a sexually transmitted disease — a problem they may not wish to address at that time;
- ensuring that a full course of three doses is given;
- difficulty of evaluating and monitoring vaccine cover; and
- systems for monitoring uptake of vaccine in this age group may not operate efficiently.

Vaccination of infants

The advantage of this approach is that parents would accept vaccination of infants against HBV infection together with other childhood vaccinations without reference to sexual behaviour.

The disadvantages of this approach are:

- it is unclear whether immunity would remain until exposure occurred in later life (this is likely to become less of a problem as more people are vaccinated, thus reducing the chance of exposure to infection);

- introduction of a further childhood vaccination would reduce the 'uptake' of the others. This problem would be avoided if HBV vaccine could be delivered as a combined vaccine also containing the diphtheria, pertussis, tetanus (DPT) vaccine; such preparations are under evaluation.

Vaccination of infants is preferable to vaccination of adolescents as there are sufficient mechanisms to ensure, monitor and evaluate cover. A booster dose could be given in early adolescence, combined with a health education package. A rolling programme could be introduced, giving priority to urban areas.

Production of hepatitis B vaccines by recombinant DNA techniques

Recombinant DNA (rDNA) techniques have been used to express HBsAg and hepatitis core antigen in prokaryotic cells (eg *Escherichia coli* and *Bacillus subtilis*) and in eukaryotic cells (eg mutant mouse LM cells, HeLa cells, COS cells, Chinese hamster ovary (CHO) cells, and yeast cells (*Saccharomyces cerevisiae*)).

Recombinant yeast HBV vaccines are safe, antigenic and free of side-effects (apart from minor local reactions in a small number of recipients). Immunogenicity is similar in general terms to that of the plasma-derived vaccine. Recombinant yeast HBV vaccines are now in use in many countries. A vaccine based on HBsAg expressed in mammalian (CHO) cells is in use in the People's Republic of China, and vaccines produced in cell cultures using viral vectors such as vaccinia are under evaluation.

Hepatitis B antibody escape mutants

Although the subtype of HBsAg varies in different geographical isolates of the virus, all share a common group antigenic determinant, *a*. Production of antibodies to this epitope appears to mediate cross-protection against all subtypes, as demonstrated by challenge with a second subtype of the virus following recovery from an initial experimental infection. The epitope *a* is located in the region of amino acids 124–148 of the major surface protein, and appears to have a double loop conformation. A monoclonal antibody recognising a region within this *a* epitope is capable of neutralising the infectivity of HBV for chimpanzees. Competitive inhibition assays using the same monoclonal antibody demonstrate that equivalent antibodies are present in serum samples from subjects immunised with either plasma-derived or recombinant HBV vaccine.

In a study of the immunogenicity and efficacy of HBV vaccines in Italy, a number of individuals who had apparently mounted a successful immune response and became anti-HBs-positive, later became infected with HBV. These cases were characterised by the co-existence of non-complexed anti-HBs and HBsAg, and in 32 of 44 vaccinated subjects there were other markers of HBV infection. Furthermore, analysis of the antigen using monoclonal antibodies suggested that the *a* epitope was either absent or masked by antibody. Subsequent sequence analysis of the virus from one of these cases revealed a mutation in the nucleotide sequence encoding the *a* epitope — the consequence of which was a substitution of arginine for glycine at amino-acid 145.

There is now considerable evidence for a wide geographical distribution of this point mutation in HBV from guanosine to adenosine at position 587, resulting in an amino-acid substitution at position 145 from glycine to arginine in the highly antigenic group determinant *a* of the surface antigen. This stable mutation has been found in viral isolates from children several years later, and has been described in Italy, Singapore, Japan and Brunei. It has also been described in the USA, Germany and the UK in liver transplant recipients infected with HBV who had been treated with specific HBIG or humanised HBV monoclonal antibody.

The region in which this mutation occurs is an important virus epitope to which vaccine-induced neutralising antibody binds (as discussed above), and the mutant virus is not specifically neutralised by this antibody. It can replicate as a competent virus, implying that the amino-acid substitution does not alter virus attachment to the hepatocyte. This has been confirmed in experimental transmission studies by Purcell and his colleagues at the US National Institutes of Health (awaiting publication).

In a study currently in progress at Singapore, three groups of babies have been immunised against HBV:

- 50 born to mothers without HBsAg;
- 600 born to mothers with HBsAg but without *e* antigen; and
- 600 born to mothers with HBsAg and *e* antigen.

The first two groups were immunised successfully, but there were 40 vaccine failures in the third group, and they all possessed HBsAg and core antibody. Direct sequencing has been completed for 26 isolates from these 40 infants:

- 15 had wild-type sequences and serological profiles usually indicating *in utero* infection; and
- 11 had variant sequences — the 145 glycine-to-arginine variant alone (4), with other changes (2), alanine at position 144 (1 twin) or other changes not yet evaluated.[10]

Variants of HBV with altered antigenicity of the envelope protein show that HBV is not as antigenically singular as previously believed and that humoral escape mutation can occur *in vivo*. There are two causes for concern:

- failure to detect HBsAg may lead to transmission through donated blood or organs; and
- HBV may infect individuals who become anti-HBs positive after immunisation.

Variation in the second loop of the *a* determinant seems especially important. Mutant variants, altered genotypes, and unusual strains are now being sought in many laboratories.[11]

The emergence of antibody escape mutants is therefore a major concern and may necessitate future modification of current HBV vaccines.

Hepatitis B vaccines containing pre-S epitopes

A disadvantage of plasma-derived and recombinant HBV vaccines containing only the major protein of HBsAg (without pre-S sequences) is the lack of immune responsiveness in at least 5–10% of healthy recipients ('non-responders'). The identification of an immunodominant domain in the pre-S2 region of HBsAg[12], and the observation that mice immunologically non-responsive to the major HBsAg protein make antibodies to a synthetic peptide corresponding to this epitope[13,14], stimulated interest in the incorporation of pre-S sequences into HBV vaccines. Itoh *et al.*[15] demonstrated that after coupling to keyhole limpet haemocyanin, a synthetic peptide encompassing 19 amino acids from the pre-S2 region elicited a protective antibody response when administered to chimpanzees. The middle (pre-S2+S) and large (pre-S1+pre-S2+S) forms of HBsAg have been expressed in yeast using constitutive and inducible promoters, respectively.[16,17] The former preparation has been evaluated for safety and immunogenicity[18] A vaccine containing all three forms of HBsAg (large, middle and major) synthesised in CHO cells, has been tested in Singapore. The preparation proved safe and immunogenic, and produced a rapid antibody response in 96% of the recipients.[19]

Hybrid virus vaccines

Potential live vaccines using recombinant vaccinia viruses have been constructed for HBV (also for herpes simplex, rabies and other viruses). Foreign viral DNA is introduced into the vaccinia viral genome by construction of chimaeric genes and homologous recombination in cells; the large size of the genome of vaccinia virus (185,000 base pairs) precludes gene insertion *in vitro*. A chimaeric gene consisting of vaccinia virus promoter sequences, ligated to the coding sequence for the desired foreign protein, is flanked by vaccinia virus DNA in a plasmid vector.

The recloned vaccinia virus containing HBsAg sequences has been used successfully for 'priming' experimental animals. The advantages of vaccinia virus recombinant as a vaccine include:

- low cost;
- ease of administration by multiple pressure or by the scratch technique;
- vaccine stability;
- long shelf-life; and
- the possible use of polyvalent antigens.

Adverse reactions with vaccinia virus vaccines are well documented and their incidence and severity must be carefully weighed against the adverse reactions associated with existing vaccines which any new recombinant vaccine might replace. The reports of spread of current strains of vaccinia virus to contacts may also present difficulties. Other recombinant viruses used as vectors are being explored — including oral adenovirus vaccines which have been in use for about 20 years.[20]

Novel hepatitis B vaccines using hybrid particles

Other developments include the use of HBsAg in a particulate form by expressing the proteins in mammalian cells. In-phase insertions of variable length and sequence of another virus (poliomyelitis virus type I) were made in different regions of the S gene of HBV. The envelope proteins carrying the surface antigen and the insert are assembled with cellular lipids in the cultured mammalian cells after transfection. The inserted polio neutralisation peptide was found to be exposed on the surface of the hybrid envelope particles and to induce neutralising antibodies against poliovirus in mice immunised experimentally. This approach may also be useful for studying the biological activity of other peptides incorporated into the surface of an organised multimolecular complex.

In addition to HBV, another potentially excellent carrier vehicle for human vaccines incorporates core particles of HBV, which can be produced readily by rDNA techniques. The advantage of the core structure as a particle includes its ability, first, to induce an antibody with approximately 100-fold greater efficiency than the surface antigen particle and, secondly, to augment T-helper cell function. The feasibility of this approach was demonstrated with synthetic peptides of foot and mouth disease virus after fusion to HBV core.[21]

Chemically synthesised hepatitis B vaccines

The development of chemically synthesised polypeptide vaccines offers many advantages in attaining the ultimate goal of producing chemically uniform, safe and cheap viral immunogens to replace many current vaccines. The latter often contain large quantities of irrelevant microbial antigen determinants, proteins and other material in addition to the essential immunogen required for the induction of protective antibody.[20,22] The preparation of antibodies against viral proteins using fragments of chemically synthesised peptides mimicking viral amino-acid sequences is now a possible and attractive alternative approach in immunoprophylaxis.[23]

Successful mimicking of determinants of HBsAg using chemically synthesised peptides in linear and cyclical forms has been reported by several groups of investigators. Peptides have been synthesised which retain biological function and appropriate secondary structure, even though they either have a limited sequence homology with the natural peptide or are much smaller.

Various other studies also confirm that selected overlapping peptides corresponding to relevant epitopes of HBsAg may be useful as synthetic vaccines; when combined with adjuvants and antisera, these peptides cross-react with the native surface antigen particles, and protective immunity has been demonstrated in limited experimental studies in animals.

Enhancement of the immunogenicity of the pre-S region of HBsAg has been demonstrated in mice using chemically synthesised amino-acid residues. The immune response to the pre-S2 region was shown to be regulated by H-2 linked genes distinct from those which regulate the response to the S region. It was also demonstrated that immunisation of a 'non-responder' murine strain with particles containing both S and pre-S2 can circumvent non-responsiveness. More recently, a protein sequence which mediates attachment of HBV to human hepatoma cells was identified. A synthetic peptide analogue, recognised by both cell receptors and viral antibodies, elicited antibodies reacting with the virus. Such a preparation may elicit protective antibodies by blocking the attachment of virus to cells.

Designing proteins with the correct structure and with functional activities is, however, exceedingly difficult because it is not possible to predict the tertiary structure of a protein from its amino-acid sequence alone. X-ray crystallography and interactive computer graphics are essential, and the available tools require further refining.

Synthetic peptides may therefore be employed in due course as vaccines, although mixtures of more than one peptide may be required. Many questions remain to be answered, but the critical issues are whether antibodies induced by synthetic immunogens will be protective, and whether protective immunity will persist. Some of the carrier proteins and adjuvants that have been linked to the synthetic molecules cannot be used in man; it is essential to find acceptable and safe material for covalent linkage or, alternatively, to synthesise sequences which do not require linkage.

Acknowledgements

Much of the work described in this chapter has been carried out in collaboration with Dr TJ Harrison, Dr JN Zuckerman (HAV vaccines) and others. The laboratory studies were supported by the Violet Richards Charitable Trust, WHO, SmithKline Beecham Biologicals and Immuno Ltd. The work on the HAV strain LSH/Syme was supported by SCLAVO Spa.

References

1. Provost PJ, Hilleman MR. An inactivated hepatitis A virus vaccine prepared from infected marmoset liver. *Proceedings of the Society for Experimental Biology and Medicine* 1975; **159:** 201–13
2. Provost PJ, Hilleman MR. Preparation of human hepatitis A virus in cell culture *in vitro*. *Proceedings of the Society for Experimental Biology and Medicine* 1979; **160:** 213–21
3. Ellis RW, Provost PJ. Hepatitis B and A vaccines. In: Zuckerman AJ (ed). *Recent developments in prophylactic immunization*. Dordecht: Kluwer Academic Publishers, 1989: 181–209
4. Shaw FE Jr, Guess IJA, Roets JM, Mohr FE, *et al*. Effect of anatomic site, age and smoking on the immune response to hepatitis B vaccination. *Vaccine* 1989; **7:** 425–30
5. Baer GM, Fishbein DR. Rabies post-exposure prophylaxis. *New England Journal of Medicine* 1987; **316:** 1270–1

6. Cockcroft A, Soper P, Insail C, Kennard Y, *et al.* Antibody response after hepatitis B immunisation in health care workers. *British Journal of Industrial Medicine* 1990; **47:** 199–202

7. Zuckerman JN, Cockcroft A, Zuckerman AJ. Site of injection for vaccination. *British Medical Journal* 1992; **305:** 1158

8. Zuckerman AJ. Who should be immunised against hepatitis B? *British Medical Journal* 1984; **289:** 1243–4

9. Deinhardt FD, Zuckerman AJ. Immunization against hepatitis B: Report on a WHO meeting on viral hepatitis in Europe. *Journal of Medical Virology* 1985; **17:** 209–17

10. Zuckerman AJ, Harrison TJ, Oon C-J. Mutations in S region of hepatitis B virus. *Lancet* 1994; **343:** 737–8

11. Carman WF, Thomas H, Zuckerman AJ, Harrison T. Molecular variants of hepatitis B virus. In: Zuckerman AJ, Howard HC (eds). *Viral hepatitis: scientific basis and clinical management.* Edinburgh: Churchill Livingstone, 1993: 115–36

12. Neurath AR, Kent SBH, Strick N. Location and chemical synthesis of a pre-S gene coded immunodominant epitope of hepatitis B virus. *Science* 1984; **224:** 392–5

13. Neurath AR, Kent SBH, Strick N, Stark D, Sproul P. Genetic restriction of immune responsiveness to synthetic peptides corresponding to sequences in the pre-S region of the hepatitis B virus (HBV) envelope. *Journal of Medical Virology* 1985; **17:** 119–25

14. Milich DR, Thornton GB, Neurath AR, Kent SB, *et al.* Enhanced immunogenicity of the pre-S region of hepatitis B surface antigen. *Science* 1985; **228:** 1195–9

15. Itoh Y, Takai E, Ohnuma, Kitajima K, *et al.* A synthetic peptide vaccine involving the product of the pre-S(2) region of hepatitis B virus DNA: protective efficacy in chimpanzees. *Proceedings of the National Academy of Science USA* 1986; **83:** 9174–8

16. Ellis RW, Kniskerm PJ, Hagopian A, Schultz LD, *et al.* Preparation and testing of a recombinant-derived hepatitis B vaccine consisting of pre-S2 + S polypeptides. In: Zuckerman AJ (ed). *Viral hepatitis and liver disease.* New York: Alan R Liss Inc., 1988: 1079–86

17. Kniskern PJ, Hagopian A, Burke P, Dunn N, *et al.* A candidate vaccine for hepatitis B containing the complete viral surface protein. *Hepatology* 1988; **8:** 82–7

18. Miskivsky E, Gershman K, Clements ML, Cupps T, *et al.* Comparative safety and immunogenicity of yeast recombinant hepatitis B vaccines containing S-antigens and pre-S2-S antigens. *Vaccine* 1991; **9:** 346–50

19. Yap L, Guan R, Chan SH. Recombinant DNA hepatitis B vaccine containing pre-S components of the HBV coat protein — a preliminary study of immunogenicity. *Vaccine* 1992; **10:** 439–42

20. Zuckerman AJ. Immunization against hepatitis B. *British Medical Bulletin* 1990; **46:** 383–98

21. Clarke BE, Newton SE, Carrol AR, Francis MJ, *et al.* Improved immunogenicity of a peptide epitope after fusion to hepatitis B core protein. *Nature* 1987; **330:** 381–4

22. Zuckerman AJ. Synthetic hepatitis B vaccine. *Nature* 1973; **241:** 499

23. Lerner RA, Green N, Alexander H, Liu FT, *et al.* Chemically

synthesized peptides predicted from the nucleotide sequence of hepatitis B virus genome elicit antibodies reactive with the native envelope protein of Dane particles. *Proceedings of the National Academy of Science USA* 1981; **78:** 3403–7

INDEX

Headings and page references to chapters are given in bold type.